# FAITH HEALING

# FAITH HEALING

## The Religious Experience as a Therapeutic Process

*By*

### AILON SHILOH

*Department of Anthropology*
*University of South Florida*
*Tampa, Florida*

CHARLES C THOMAS • PUBLISHER

*Springfield • Illinois • U.S.A.*

*Published and Distributed Throughout the World by*
CHARLES C THOMAS • PUBLISHER
2600 South First Street
Springfield, Illinois 62717, U.S.A.

© *1981, by* CHARLES C THOMAS • PUBLISHER
ISBN 0-398-04509-7
Library of Congress Catalog Card Number: 81-8993

*With THOMAS BOOKS careful attention is given to all details of
manufacturing and design. It is the Publisher's desire to present books that are
satisfactory as to their physical qualities and artistic possibilities and
appropriate for their particular use. THOMAS BOOKS will be true to those
laws of quality that assure a good name and good will.*

*Printed in the United States of America*
I-RX-1

Library of Congress Cataloging in Publication Data

Shiloh, Ailon.
   Faith healing.

   Bibliography: p.
   Includes index.
   1. Spiritual healing.  I. Title.
BT732.5.S52   615.8'52   81-8993
ISBN 0-398-04509-7      AACR2

This book is dedicated to the scholars and students,
healers and healed, who, over the centuries,
have provided material for this study.

# PREFACE

PRIOR to Columbus, the mapmakers of Europe wrote *Ne Plus Ultra* — "There is no more" — at the beginning of the Straits of Gibraltar, opening to the Atlantic Ocean. That was the end of the world; definite and certain, there was no more.

After the voyages of Columbus, and the initiation of the incredible discoveries, these European mapmakers began to have some comprehension of the magnitude of their error. The closed-in, circumscribed, medieval-minded Europeans were beginning to receive hints and glimmers of the wonders of the New World, of the entire world, and of the marvellous potential that lay before them.

The mapmakers returned to their maps and they erased the word *Ne*. The phrase now stood as *Plus Ultra* — "There is more!" they declared, "There is more!"

This term is perhaps not inappropriate as the theme of this book. I herein attempt to describe and analyze, delineate, and structure factors essential to one of the most significant phenomenon attendant to human existence — the circumstances of faith healing. For over thirty years I have studied this phenomenon around the world. Cross-culturally — I mean by that whether I was working among American Indians, North Chinese farmers, South Vietnamese city folk, Christian Arab villagers, Muslim Nigerian traders, or middle-class Americans in the megalopolis — I have everywhere found widespread manifestations of faith healing.

This book is intended to be an objective, but sympathetic, description and analysis of (1) certain of the circumstances attendant to faith healing actions; (2) considerations of the methods by which faith healing seems to function most effectively; and (3) for whom (which type of persons) faith healing seems to operate most effectively.

In order to develop my reasoning in as clear a manner as possible, I have written a series of forty short and challenging chapters. Each chapter is meant to operate as a distinct but integral factor in this overall study. In the development of my reasoning, I have constructed a paradigm that, per my analysis, operates to interpret certain of the dynamics of faith healing. The appropriate setting; a "cloud of witnesses"; the right healer; the healee, who truly wishes to be healed (never a given); and the public confession — I delineate and structure these as critical stages necessary to optimal faith healing.

The actual faith healing occurrence, I propose, is really a classic demonstration of "telescoped time therapy." In a matter of moments — suddenly and dramatically, visibly and forcefully — a healing can actually take place. For the healer, the healee, and the witnesses, this is a moment of supreme emotion and pure ecstacy.

As a medical anthropologist I make no claims or judgments, authorize no beliefs, and give no ridicule. My task is to try to describe and analyze the phenomenon in as objective and rational a manner as possible. I certainly have no illusions as to the inadequacies and limitations of this work. This is not a "how-to" book. It makes no promises and no guarantees. It raises many questions and proposes only a few tentative answers.

I hope that each reader of this book will find the material to be personally meaningful and with potential personal consideration and application. This book will, I hope, stimulate others to initiate additional and improved theories, investigations, and analyses.

This work should be important to those concerned with health and ill-health, sickness and suffering, and pain and death. These will affect all of us at one time or another. Those grappling with the complexities of "spontaneous remission," "placebo," and "mind-over-body" control should find this material to be of significance. Those involved in faith and religion, soul and spirit, sin and punishment, and confession and salvation will discover herein critical issues and challenges.

Faith healing is a human phenomenon that should neither be crassly dismissed nor blindly accepted. Faith healing needs to be studied rationally and scientifically, with carefully controlled and recorded documentation and verification.

"There is more!" I assure you, "There is more!"

A. S.

# ACKNOWLEDGMENTS

THIS book represents the distillation of over thirty years of field work study and research — investigating, reasoning, postulating, testing.

If this book has any value it is due to the cooperation of hundreds of courteous persons around the world who permitted me to be with them in their most personal moments of pain and suffering, to attend with them their healing services, and to witness their triumphs and tragedies.

I acknowledge their strengths, and I hope that this book can be of some help to them and their children.

# CONTENTS

# FAITH HEALING

# "I FELT AS THOUGH I HAD BEEN RAPED!"

A university professor in her forties transferred from a secure and pleasant northern university to a new and growing southern university. "I thought that the change would be good," she told me.

Within six months after her move, when all relations with her previous university had been officially sundered, she realized that her new department chairman was a mild psychopath, the type that obtains an almost sexual pleasure out of wielding power, that almost enjoys being mean and nagging, and that officiously and carefully keeps within the letter of the law.

The chairman demanded absolute obedience and performance under penalty of constant harassment and aggravation, and gossip and innuendo. The chairman threatened the professor with dismissal for incompetence.

All attempts to resolve the situation led to emotional scenes, which were acutely unpleasant to the professor but obviously quite pleasant to the chairman. All attempts to meet with the Dean of the college, the chairman's superior, were rebuffed. "The Dean," it was announced, "supported his chairmen."

There was no union to turn to and, despite the terrible pressure, the professor was reluctant to make it a public scene, which is exactly what the chairman counted on. ·

Matters continued to deteriorate, particularly when the professor learned that her chairman was receiving treatment

3

for certain emotional problems. The professor realized that she had voluntarily backed into a destructive situation. She met again with her superior, who made it clear to her that the impasse would be resolved only when she, the professor, would publicly admit her errors, acknowledge her inferiority, and promise to mend her ways.

After duly agonizing over the alternatives, the professor did all that the department chairman commanded. "I felt as though I had been raped!" the professor recalled.

A month later she began to urinate blood. Physicians diagnosed her problem as cancer of the bladder. She was dead six months later.

Simonton et al. (1978, pp. 62-63) report on the case of a forty-year-old widow who was diagnosed with advanced cancer of the kidney. Her husband had died a year earlier and had left her to run the ranch. Exploratory surgery on the woman revealed that her cancer had spread to the extent that additional surgery and radiation therapy would be of limited value. She was sent home to die.

Once back home, she fell in love with one of her ranch hands, and they married. Despite that medical prognosis of imminent death, she led a full and active life for the next five years. Then her second husband, having run through all of her money, left her.

Within a few weeks the woman had a "major recurrence" of the cancer and died.

Lawrence Galton (1979, p. 20) reports on the case of a hard working, long-suffering, midwestern housewife who for twenty years cared for her mentally retarded daughter. She took it quietly when the daughter died.

Then, only a few months later, another daughter married against her wishes and cut herself off from the family. The mother took that silently also.

A few months later, the mother, never sick, collapsed and was dead of cancer within a month.

# "NOW I CAN BREATHE . . . "

MISS Mississippi, Cheryl Prewitt, who was told eleven years previously that she would never walk again, was crowned Miss America for 1980 (*The New Haven Register*, September 9, 1980, p. 2).

When she was eleven years old, Miss Prewitt was badly hurt in an automobile accident. Her left leg was crushed; it took one hundred stitches to help put it back together. Doctors told her parents that she would never walk again.

However, she reported, several years later she went to a revival meeting. At the climax of the faith healing service, her crippled left leg suddenly straightened out. The leg "grew" two inches instantaneously. It was a "miracle of God," she said.

Morris Cerullo, evangelist and faith healer, published a report in his magazine, *Deeper Life*, about twelve-year-old Danny Peeler.

Danny stated that he had suffered from bronchial asthma from his day of birth. During one bad attack, Danny's left lung deflated. Physicians could not inflate it. The boy suffered chronic pain, difficulty in breathing and sleeping, and acute proneness to pneumonia.

Suddenly, at a Morris Cerullo faith healing service, Danny Peeler was healed. "I felt my deflated left lung raise up completely as it filled with air! It just raised up! I could feel it! Now I can breathe without hurting anymore."

5

Danny Peeler and His mother, Elva, provided X rays to show that Danny's lungs are now "clear and completely aerated" (*Deeper Life,* July-August, 1979, p. 2).

Nicholas M. Regush, in his book *Frontiers of Medicine* (1977, p. 79), summarizes a medical report of "spontaneous recovery" by a religious healer.

The patient complained of "severe internal pains." She was operated on, and a chronic cancerous state with advanced infiltration was seen. The surgeon decided that the condition was inoperable and sewed her up. She was sent home to die.

The woman went to a faith healer. She claimed that she had been healed. She claimed that the pains disappeared, that the cancer symptoms went away. At any rate, she didn't die. She continued her normal life. Two years later, for a different reason, this woman was admitted into the same hospital for abdominal surgery. The same physician operated on her.

The medical history was before him, just as was her opened abdomen. The physician could not understand how this could be the same woman who — two years previously — he had diagnosed with inoperable cancer. There was no sign of cancer in the woman. The fleshy, spreading, cancerous, mass had completely disappeared.

# DR. ALEXIS CARREL, NOBEL PRIZE

IN the year 1903, Marie Bailly, age twenty-two, was dying of tubercular peritonitis. Despite the fact that she suffered constantly in acute pain, she begged to be taken to Lourdes. Her physician, in final desperation, agreed to permit this. He also agreed to accompany her.

She was under his direct observation all the time on the Lourdes-bound train. When they arrived there, the Medical Bureau confirmed the diagnosis; Marie Bailly could die at any moment. She was too weak to be immersed in the waters of Lourdes. Instead, she was only rubbed twice with the holy waters. A few minutes later she began to look better. Throughout that afternoon her condition improved progressively and markedly. By 7:30 that evening she was sitting up in bed.

Marie Bailly died thirty-four years later at the age of fifty-seven.

Her physician was so impressed with this healing that he became a believer. It cost him his future at the Lyons Faculty of Medicine. The physician, Alexis Carrel, joined the Rockefeller Institute for Medical Research and was awarded a Nobel Prize in 1913. His record of this event, *Journey to Lourdes*, is the best known of all of his published works.

7

# BERNADETTE OF LOURDES

FOR the true believer, a cave near Lourdes is the meeting place of Heaven and Earth. During the year of 1858, the Mother of God, the Queen of Heaven, the Virgin Mary came down to Lourdes in person. It is her presence that still overwhelms the cave. To her medium, Bernadette, she gave the powers of vision, prophecy, and healing.

Mary of the Immaculate Conception caused a spring to gush forth from this cave, a spring whose waters possess miraculous powers for healing. Plunged into these waters, bathed in them, massaged with them, and drinking of them, the dying have been given new life. The deaf and the dumb have been restored to speech and hearing. The blind have been given sight; the lame made whole; the sick healed.

Over a million persons a year make the pilgrimage to Lourdes. Miraculous healings are claimed to occur regularly, even daily. It is claimed that no one ever goes away in despair, not even the uncured. All are filled with renewed faith, hope, strength, and endurance. "The trip to Lourdes is never in vain."

Lourdes is located along the Gave River in southwestern France. It acquired fame in 1858 when a fourteen-year-old girl name Bernadette Subirous (1844-1879) related that the Virgin Mother had come down to Earth and spoken wih her on eighteen separate occasions while Bernadette was at the cave by the river. After the first visions, crowds began to go with Bernadette to the cave, but only she ever saw the Mother of God. During one vision, Bernadette was instructed to dig down for water. She did so and a spring gushed forth.

This spring flows at a rate of some 32,000 gallons a day. As the people came to the cave to pray, drink the water, and bathe in it, cures began to be claimed. By now, there are hundreds of thousands of claimed healings. Most of the claimed healings take place at Lourdes. Some occur even before the pilgrim arrives there. Others occur after the sick have returned home.

The International Medical Commission in Paris, established to investigate and authenticate these healings, has designated only fifty-four healings as "miraculous."

Bernadette Subirous, an illiterate girl of poverty-stricken parents, suffered all her life from, among other ailments, chronic asthma. She entered a convent at the age of twenty-two, and she died there when she was thirty-five. She, herself, never made any healing claims, and she never profited from the events.

# BY THE WATERS OF ST. WINEFRIDE

NOW these types of mind-body stories are not uncommon. Virtually every person now reading this book can come up with at least one or two personal experiences whereby emotional strains led to physical problems and mental stress resulted in body ailment. The blinding headache the night before a critical job interview, the upset stomach the morning of a final examination, or the heart palpitations after an unpleasant family quarrel — most of us are familiar with such negative mind-over-body controls.

Conversely, many of us are also familiar with positive mind-over-body control. We have heard of, if we have not personally experienced, cases wherein sickness, pain, and suffering were reported to have been healed by faith healing experiences, howsoever these religious experiences are defined. Unfortunately, many of these reports are of a subjective nature: personal, impressionistic, emotional, and anecdotal. They lead themselves to possible exaggeration. They are rarely documented or verified by medical authorities. Such healings may be claimed by frauds and charlatans. They may be believed by the naive and the gullible. They may be downright lies.

How can we recognize "true" faith healing? How do we distinguish "honest" faith healers from "cheats?"

We are reminded of the Chapel of St. Winefride at Holywell, Flintshire, in Wales. Winefride was a seventeenth century virgin who died defending her honor. Miraculously, she was brought back to life. Where her head had lain, while she was dead, a spring began to flow.

The crippled, maimed, deformed, and sick went to that spring to be immersed in the holy waters and to be healed. Around the chapel were stacked the crutches and surgical appliances discarded by the crippled who were healed by the holy waters.

During World War I, in 1917, the spring ran dry. It was considered essential for war morale to maintain the flowing of the waters, so a pipe was laid to the spring from a nearby reservoir used to supply water for a textile mill. The spring continued to flow, pilgrimages continued, and cures were reported, thanks to water from the Urban District Council.

# EVITA!

SICKNESS and suffering and healing and curing — these are not necessarily simple biological phenomena.

Witnesses can still be rallied to testify to the healing powers of Aimee Semple McPherson (1890-1944). A widow of Semple and divorced from McPherson, this missionary crisscrossed the United States eight times between 1918 and 1923 converting and curing thousands of sinners. She built a Temple in Los Angeles and developed her gospel that Christ is The Savior and The Healer. In 1922, she made her first religious broadcast. Despite her 1926 mysterious "kidnapping," she was a widely known and well-respected American religious healer, well within the tradition of female religious healers.

To this day, "Evita" (Eva Peron, 1919-1952), wife of the former Argentinian ruler, is believed to have possessed the powers of a healer. To this day there are those who claim to have been healed by Evita's touch or Evita's look.

Father Pio (1887-1968), while an adolescent, suffered from poor health. He became a priest but, during World War I, was drafted to serve in the Italian Army.

On September 20, 1918, Father Pio began to bleed from the wounds of Jesus — at the hands, the feet, the side. The stigmata continued at regular intervals for the rest of his life, almost fifty years. Numerous physicians examined Father Pio and attested to his bleedings. People flocked to Father Pio — for confession, baptism, and marriage. He became known as a healer, and numerous testimonials swore to his wonderful powers.

On September 6, 1956, for example, a crippled girl attended his Mass. Her bones were atrophied. Father Pio blessed her as he went by. Suddenly she leaped from her chair, in which she had been carried into church, and kissed his hand. She was completely healed.

When Father Pio died, at the age of 81, over 3,000 priests and 100,000 laymen attended his funeral. Two healing miracles were announced to have taken place as his dead body was carried by.

The National Institute of Mental Health gave over one and a quarter million dollars to study a variety of California therapies — the encounter groups, health camps, and therapy sessions — that claimed healing powers.

Findings were that such therapies benefited perhaps one-third of those attending. It provided those individuals with a sense of group belonging; it gave them social acceptance. Fears of loneliness were decreased, and self-image and self-confidence were improved. The California therapies, it was concluded, seemed to help improve personal well-being and personal adjustment. These, in turn, seemed to work positively to help improve personal health. In that sense, then, there certainly were healings.

# KAFKA'S TUBERCULOSIS

THE converse can also operate. Sickness and death, rather than health and life, may be the goal.

In his youth, Franz Kafka was engaged to be married. Yet, although claiming to be deeply in love, Kafka recorded in his diary on August 20, 1916, for example, of his profound self-doubts. If he became married, Kafka wrote, he feared that he might lose his powers of "coherence" and his ability to "concentrate."

A year later, Kafka began to cough blood. He had few illusions. He said the blood was psychic, that it was to save him from marriage. After the agonies of insomnia, wrote Kafka, now, despite his coughing blood, he was finally beginning to sleep soundly.

In September of 1917, Kafka told his lifelong friend, and later biographer, Max Brod, that the wedding was off. Clearly, now that Kafka was ill, he could no longer consider marriage. Kafka read Kierkegaard, studied the Bible, learned Hebrew, and prepared for death. Marriage, with anyone, was of no possible consideration.

On June 3, 1924, Kafka died of tuberculosis — unmarried. To the end, however, a writer in full command of his powers of "coherence" and ability to "concentrate" (from Brod, 1960).

# YOU CAN DIE FROM A BROKEN HEART

CARDIOVASCULAR diseases, including stroke, account for some 55 percent of all deaths in the United States. Cancer terminates the lives of another 25 percent. The remaining 20 percent of deaths in America are attributed to accidents, suicide and homicide (mainly among the young), influenza and pneumonia (mainly among the elderly), and cirrhosis of the liver (mainly, but not only, among heavy drinkers).

These rates, of course, are greatly affected by age, sex, and ethnic group. For example, three of every four deaths among American males between the ages of fifteen and twenty-five are caused by accidents, suicide, and homicide.

In general, in America, women live longer than men, the educated live longer than the uneducated, the rich live longer than the poor, whites live longer than blacks (but Asiatics may live longer than whites), and the married live far longer than nonmarried. According to Lynch (1977) mortality rates for all causes of death are consistently higher for divorced, single, and widowed persons of both sexes and all races.

Obviously, your personal health habits are also very important.

All else being equal, however, if you are white, male, and divorced, you are two times more likely to get lung cancer; four times more likely to get mouth and throat cancer; seven times more likely to get cirrhosis of the liver; ten times more likely to get tuberculosis.

15

If you are white, female, and divorced you are two times more likely to get genital cancer.

If you are nonwhite, male, and divorced, you are three times more likely to get genital cancer.

Deaths due to suicide and homicide and home and car "accidents" are significantly higher for all of these divorced groups. According to the American Council of Life Insurance, living healthy and living longer are two good reasons for getting married and staying married. Unfortunately, the divorce rate in America is accelerating at an astounding rate. The divorce rate has almost doubled in the past decade; every year more than one million marriages are ending in divorce.

Perhaps we should attach a notice to every marriage certificate: "Warning! Violation of these terms can be dangerous to your health!"

# VOODOO CAN ALSO KILL

ON the 20th of July, 1966, a twenty-two-year-old Afro-American woman was admitted to the Baltimore City Hospital. She complained of chest pains, blackouts, and difficulty in breathing.

After two weeks of being in the hospital, she told her physician that she had a serious problem and only three days left to solve it. She said that she had been born on Friday the thirteenth in the Okefenokee Swamp. She was delivered by a midwife who delivered three children that day. The midwife told the mothers that all three children were hexed: the first would die before her sixteenth birthday, the second before her twenty-first birthday, and the third (the patient) before her twenty-third birthday.

The first girl was killed in an automobile accident the day before her sixteenth birthday. The second girl was killed by a bullet during a saloon brawl while she was celebrating her twenty-first birthday. Now the patient, on the eve of her twenty-third birthday, was convinced that she was doomed to die. She did. On August 12, one day before her twenty-third birthday, she turned her face to the wall and died. The physicians at the hospital diagnosed the death as due to "primary pulmonary hypertension." It was a sound medical diagnosis that said everything, and nothing.

How shall we explain this death? The medical explanation was about as satisfactory as that of the poor victim. How can we explain the previous illnesses, sufferings, pain, and sometimes the healing, and how often only death?

17

# CANCER –
# FROM YOUR MIND TO YOUR BODY?

O NE way to begin to study these questions may be to consider claims that the mind can affect the body so negatively as to even induce cancer.

Galton (1979) states that the mind can control the body adversely and cause sickness. He argues that the manner in which a person confronts emotional problems somehow may set the stage, for example, for cancer development. Cancer patients, believes Galton, tend to be emotionally repressed and emotionally inhibited. They have no outlets for their emotional frustrations. They have no emotional release. After repeated emotional blows, says Galton, such a person begins to feel utterly helpless, in an utterly hopeless situation. The mind, as it were, "gives up."

This seems to set the stage to initiate, or promote, an already existing cancer potential.

Now clearly, environmental factors are critical to cancer development: the sun, corrosive chemicals and gases, and nuclear radiation. Clearly, personal behavioral patterns can also be critical to the promotion of cancer; heavy smoking and drinking, possibly certain drugs, and probably certain foods and their manner of preparation. There is also the genetic factor; quite possibly some persons may have a familial heritage, genetic constituents, that provide them with a predisposition to cancer development.

18

Over and above these factors, however, Galton stresses the emotional factor — the dammed-up-frustrations that can lead to cancer manifestations. Implicit in the reasoning of Galton and his colleagues is that cancer does not just occur. Cancer is not random. Cancer appears, attacks, goes wild, and destroys only when it is so permitted, even encouraged.

These are very strong charges. It can be very painful to read. This is not, I must stress, a statement of proven fact. It is, at best, a proposed explanation. It is a hypothesis yet to be tested and proven.

# THE BIG C

CANCER strikes some member of two of every three families in America. For women, the most dangerous period for a cancer attack is between the ages of thirty to fifty-five; for men the most dangerous period is from the age of fifty-five and on.

Women, in other words, tend to get their cancer during those years when they, their husbands and their children are still young, growing, and interdependent. Men, on the other hand, tend to get their cancer when they are in their postproductive years. Their careers are no longer as developing. They have peaked. Cancer for women, however, tends to come at a more dramatic, difficult, and familial-threatened time in the life cycle.

Cancer also seems to be manifesting a racial bias. According to Dr. LaSalle Leffal, president of the American Cancer Society, the number of cancer deaths in blacks is up 26 percent over the last two decades. This is about five times the increase over the same period for whites. The cancer rate for blacks, terminal and otherwise, is up 8 percent over the last quarter century. The cancer rate for whites has, over the same period, declined about 3 percent.

No wonder, however, that for all of us cancer is a feared malignancy. Cancer for some of us is so frightening that we are even afraid to speak its name, instead preferring to call it by a euphemism — the Big C.

# THE DANGEROUS D?

THERE is an old and widespread belief that you can help cause or induce your own cancer. The argument goes that pronounced negative mental attitudes — depression — can result in, among other illness, cancer. The dangerous D can lead to the big C.

Galen, the Greek physician practicing during the second century of this era, wrote that cheerful women were less prone to cancer than were women of a depressed nature.

The noted French physician, Claude Bernard, in his 1865 classic, *Experimental Medicine*, argues that physicians must recognize the body as a harmonious whole, mental as well as physical. When this harmony is disturbed, illness results. The more serious and chronic the disturbance, so also the illness. Cancer is one of the by-products of such an imbalance.

Simonton et al. (1978, p. 55) cite the concluding remark of H. Snow's 1893 study of *Cancer and the Cancer-Process*: "Of all causes of the cancer-process in every stage, neurotic agencies are the most powerful."

Lawrence LeShan is perhaps the leading advocate of the significance of the psychological life history in cancer manifestation and resolution. In his book, *You Can Fight for Your Life*, LeShan argues that a healthy mental attitude is necessary in order to conquer cancer. You need a new perspective on your life, on your problems, on your resources. You need to decide if you really want to get well, what you have to live for, and what you need to do to help yourself

21

# COWBOYS WITH WHITE HATS

SIMONTON would certainly subscribe to these reasonings.

O. Carl Simonton is a Fort Worth, Texas, physician who has had cancer twice. The first cancer was treated surgically; the second cancer was treated by the "Simonton technique."

The Simonton technique is based upon the premise that if emotional forces play an important role in helping to develop cancer, then emotional forces can be mobilized to help defeat the cancer, or at least to delay its negative course. Simonton has joined the increasing number of physicians, psychologists, and others who are recognizing that many, if not all, of our illnesses may be due to mental workings on the body. The mind is subjected to stress and strains that it perceives as unacceptable and unbearable. The mind cannot take the pressure, the body gives in and an illness develops.

Kenneth Pelletier, in his book *Mind as Healer, Mind as Slayer,* states that "all disorders are psychosomatic" in the sense that mind and body are intimately involved. Many of our illnesses today, he argues, are "afflictions of civilization" – the body responds to chronic and apparently unresolvable emotional strains.

Simonton, stemming from his time as a resident in training as a radiation therapist at the University of Oregon Medical School, noticed that the more he could get his patients

22

involved in their own care, the better they seemed to do. He began to study processes of motivating patients, deliberately arousing and involving the internal mental workings of the patient at the same time the external physical therapy was being practiced.

One of Simonton's earliest and most reported cases was that of a sixty-one-year-old man with advanced throat cancer. Simonton had the man begin daily practices of relaxation and "imaging," i.e. mentally picturing the radiation therapy as a force of tiny bullets of energy, striking and destroying the aberrant cancer cells. Then the white blood cells would come in, swarm over the dead and dying cancer cells, and flush them out of the body. Each imaging session closed with the patient visualizing his cancer tumor as steadily decreasing. His health was steadily increasing. "Within two weeks his cancer had noticeably diminished," Simonton reported later.

This success led him to develop a health team, cassettes, television tapes, lectures, and the Fort Worth Cancer Counseling and Research Center, all of which were designed to advance this "imaging" cancer therapy. This imaging therapy, incidentally, is designed to accompany the traditional program of cancer therapy. I am not aware that Simonton and his colleagues have ever advocated their imaging therapy as a replacement for orthodox medicine.

In this imaging therapy, Simonton and his colleagues have found that better results may be obtained when the patients can visualize their own body resources working for them. Operating within the culture and traditions of the Texas range, some patients visualized their medicine and radiation as cowboys with white hats charging after the cancer cells, rounding them up, and dispatching them down the urinary tract. The cowboys with white hats always won their fights with the villains. For such patients, the folklore of the West plays a critical supportive role. For other patients, the "good guys" may be represented as knights in shining armor, or hard-working scrubbing brushes, or powerful medicinal hoses.

# A CRUEL HOAX

SIMONTON and his colleagues believe that there is a cancer-prone personality. Cancer does not just occur; it develops among especially vulnerable persons. Such vulnerable persons manifest certain personality traits (such as inhibition and repression), have been subjected to a variety of emotional crises (divorce, loss of job, etc.), and have recently lost loved ones (particularly within the nuclear family of husband, wife, and children).

In a sympathetic critique of Simonton and his theory, Maggie Scarf (1980) argues that many of us, to some degree, manifest such personality traits. We have been subjected to a variety of similar emotional crises. We may have recently lost loved ones. All of us, however, do not necessarily develop cancer. These traits and events, in themselves, do not necessarily cause cancer. Furthermore, cancer may be found where these traits and events are absent. There is not an inevitable relationship and there certainly is no proven causal relationship. Maggie Scarf cites the works of Bernard Fox of the National Cancer Institute and Jimmie Holland of the Sloan-Kettering Institute for Cancer Research. Both of these scientists have found little evidence to support the reasoning that emotional responses are necessarily cancer-causing.

Robert J. Keehn, of the Medical Follow-Up Agency of the National Academy of Sciences National Research Council, studied former World War II and Korean War Prisoners — certainly persons who underwent stress — and found their

24

cancer rates to be no different from cancer rates among the population at large. Despite the long tradition and clinical data of a relationship between mind and body, depression and illness and stress and cancer, there is still not a proven causal relationship.

There is little doubt that the mind can play a critical role in causing body sickness. There is recognition that the mind can play a critical role in helping to heal the body. However, little is known about the actual functioning of the human mind and its workings on the body. We must be wary of exagerrated claims, even while we recognize the tremendous potential for good. The practice of faith healing is an example of the need for such caution.

Faith healing — the religious experience as a therapeutic process — is a very important practice. A better understanding of the forces operating in faith healing could make a significant contribution to medicine. A clearer awareness of the powers of faith healing could enrich our appreciation of religion. Improved insight into the workings of faith healing can only serve to help all of us.

It is essential, therefore, that we try to study this phenomenon as carefully as possible. Otherwise, we might find ourselves accused of the same charges being laid against Simonton and his colleagues. The arguments of Simonton and others, that the cancer patient is somehow responsible for the cancer, is being attacked by many physicians. Holland, for example, says that cancer patients have enough fear and pain. They do not need to have the additional burden that somehow their cancer is their own fault. This can be a dreadful charge. Holland accuses Simonton and his colleagues of practicing a cruel hoax.

# THE GURU IN YOUR BODY

W ITH this complex of arguments and cautions constantly before us, let us proceed, then, with our study.

Thomas Edison is quoted as saying that "the body is just something to carry the brain around in" (Lygre, 1979, p. 133). While this may seem like naive Edisoniana, Lygre cites a number of examples whereby Indian religious leaders have been able to demonstrate just how effectively the body can be and is controlled by the mind.

H. H. Swami Rama, tested at the Menninger Foundation in the late 1960s, made over one-half of his right palm 10° warmer than the other half. Electrodes were attached to his scalp and the swami proceeded to predict, and achieve, several different patterns of brain wave activity.

In an experiment conducted by the British Broadcasting Corporation in 1970, Ramanand Yogi meditated for nearly six hours inside a locked, airtight box. Scientists monitoring his oxygen consumption reported that the yogi had reduced his oxygen consumption by more than half.

Such mind over body control has also been demonstrated with other animals. Through the deliberate application of conditioning techniques, such as stimulating the pleasure-reward areas of the brain, Neal Miller and his team at the Rockefeller University in New York trained animals to mentally control involuntary bodily functions. The animals produced specific brain wave patterns; selectively dilated blood

26

vessels; and controlled heart rate, blood pressure, rate of urine formation, and rate of intestinal contractions.

There are few scientists, today, who would deny that we might be able to control far more of our internal body organs and functions than we have hitherto considered.

Andrija Puharich, writing in the Regush compilation (1977, pp. 56-70), reports that some trained Indian yogins can so control their bodies as to achieve mastery even over the gastrointestinal tract. A long bandage is swallowed, propelled through the twenty-eight feet of the gastrointestinal canal, and then expelled from the rectum. In other case demonstrations, the body rhythm can be reversed — a yogi can draw up into his bladder up to a litre of water.

These are not so much parlor tricks as they are demonstrations of how little we actually understand our mind-body relations.

If the mind can control the body in such manifest ways, then what could be achieved through even more deliberate, directed, voluntary mind control? We are, as it were, on the threshold of a new frontier, and we are dazed, even frightened, at what lies before us. Faith healing, mind-over-body control, is an old idea whose scientific time may have finally come.

Similar to those standing on an unknown shore just before the dawn, we have only a dim awareness of what lies before us, and that awareness is tempered with fear and foreboding, as well as hope and excitement. Faith healing recognizes that the guru in our body may be in our mind or elsewhere. Faith healing tests this reasoning for the best of reasons — i.e. to help us improve and maintain our health. It is an awesome challenge.

# JESUS LOVES YOU ALL

IT is now appropriate to consider faith healing as an example of how the mind can
work to help heal the body. It is useful to describe some ordinary faith healing services that have taken place around the
United States.

In New Haven, Connecticut, I attended a Catholic Workshop of Prayer and Healing. The service was held in the early
evening and in the basement of the cathedral. Some fifty of
us, men and women, ranging in age from the late thirties to
the midsixties were in attendance. A tall and well-built priest
in his midsixties appeared and led us in group singing of "Oh
What a Friend We Have in Jesus." He then talked to us about
the importance of prayer. We not only complain, grumble,
and whine to Jesus, but we must also give thanks to Jesus
when we can do a good deed; help a friend; be loving to our
spouse, understanding to our children, or respectful to our
elders. It is important to pray to Jesus and thank him for the
good things that we can do. We must not pray to Jesus only
when things are not going our way.

"Wear the cross," he urged. He himself wore a large, iron
cross hanging on his chest. "The cross will comfort you and
heal you. Look at this cross of Jesus. Study it." He held it
up. "The head of Jesus is in Heaven, where you will go if you
do good work for Jesus. The feet of Jesus are on Earth; Jesus came down to each of you to save you from Hell and to
take you up to Heaven. The arms of Jesus are stretched out

to embrace you, to help you, and to heal you. As you see, north, south, east, and west, Jesus is everywhere and loves you all. Jesus loves you all.."

He then had us hold hands and form a large circle. "This is a prayer group to Jesus to heal us. Do not worry about failure. Half of our marriages fail but we do not stop marrying. We must pray to Jesus. First, however, we must deal with our sins. We must exorcise the devil in us." We were told to close our eyes, to breathe deeply and slowly, and to whisper the name of Jesus after each breathing. We stood in a circle, eyes closed, holding hands. All that could be heard was the sound of regular deep breathing and the whispering sibilance of "Jesus."

"Now," asked the priest, "who needs healing?" He placed a chair in the center of the circle. "Who needs healing?"

A plainly dressed woman in her late thirties raised her hand and said, "I do." She went in and sat down in the chair.

"What is wrong?" the priest asked. "Tell us what is wrong with you. Tell us why you have left Jesus."

"I hate my sister. I had to take care of her when our father left us. I was too young. It was too much of a responsibility. I hate her."

The priest stood behind her. He placed his hands on her shoulders. He went on quietly. His voice was warm and supportive.

"Who else do you hate?"

"I hate my children," she sobbed. "It has spilled over to my children. I am jealous of their young happiness. They keep reminding me of what I never had."

"And what else," went on the priest.

"It has made me sick. I don't feel well. There is something growing inside me. I can feel it."

The priest placed his hands around the woman's head. He held her tightly. He called on Jesus to heal this woman.

"Oh Jesus, heal this woman's anger. Cast out her evil. Replace it with love for you. She wants to do good, Jesus, help her. She has confessed her sins, Jesus. Help her, Jesus. Help her, Jesus."

The woman began to shake, to rock in her chair. The priest held her firmly. Again he called on Jesus to heal this woman. After a while, she calmed down. She began to cry.

"Oh sweet Jesus," she sobbed. "Thank you, thank you."

The priest then took holy oil and annointed her forehead, eyes, and mouth.

Then a man in his fifties came forward with complaints of bad eyesight, a woman asked for healing of her arthritic pain, and another woman asked for help with her son's ingratitude. Similar procedures were followed; there were confessions of personal anguish, jealousy, fear, and pain. There were requests for forgiveness and promises to repent. Jesus was called upon to forgive these repenting sinners. Jesus was asked to heal them of their ailments. The applicants confessed, shook, sobbed, and cried with relief. They claimed to "feel better," to be "relieved," "to be refreshed," and to be "healed."

By the end of these healings we all felt tired and drained of physical and emotional energy. The priest then had us close our eyes, breathe regularly, and call on Jesus. We then sang a song of thanks to Jesus, prayed a prayer, and the healing service was over.

# HATE CAN MAKE YOU SICK

IN St. Petersburg, Florida, I attended a "Spiritual Healing Service and Workshop." The leader, we were told, was formerly a devout Baptist minister from Georgia whose wife had suddenly left him.

"The minister left the pulpit and turned to evil — women, drink, and drugs, the whole lot." Then one night he again found Jesus. He confessed his sins; he promised to do good.

"Jesus healed him and sent him out to heal others."

After these introductory remarks, the reborn minister appeared. He was a portly gentleman in his late forties. He led us in singing and in prayer. He then began to preach.

"Hate," he declared, "hate can make you sick. Don't think about what your hate is doing to the other fellow. Think about what it is doing to you. Hate can make you sick."

He looked hard at us.

"Hate is like a poison. The more you hate someone, the more poison there is in your body. Don't think you are getting even — you are getting sick. Your hate can kill — you."

The minister looked around the hall.

"How many of you came here to be healed?" he asked.

Over half of the audience of some eighty persons raised their hands.

"Well, God cannot heal when you're full of hate. Hate blocks God's healing. You have got to get rid of your hate. Greed, envy, and jealousy — these are all forms of hate.

31

You hate someone who you think has something that you want. Got cannot help you until you exorcise this hate. Stand up, all of you who want to be healed!" he commanded.

"Who is the one person that you most hate? Think hard now. Who is the one person that you really hate? Who is really making you sick? Say the name! Say it out loud! Shout it! Again! Get it out of you. That hate is making you sick. That hate will kill you. God cannot heal you until you get rid of this hate. You must forgive."

(At about this time I remembered a remark by William Sloane Coffin, Jr., the former Yale chaplain: "When you think about your enemy, think about what you have done to earn that enmity.")

The hall resounded with persons shouting out names: many were smiling, others crying, and some were doing both.

"Now," declared the minister, "now God can begin to heal you."

# CONFESSION IS GOOD FOR THE BODY

THIS was a healing service in Washington, D. C. We were in the auditorium of a large downtown hotel. The healer was a lay religious leader from North Carolina. He had been a prosperous banker until one night Jesus appeared to him.

"Jesus told me to go out and heal the sick."

The former banker obeyed the instruction and was now a poor, itinerant healer.

There was a pervasive air of expectancy in the room. Over half of the audience of some seventy persons were standing, arms upraised, with a look of patient hope on their faces. It was as though they knew that God would answer their prayers. The scene might remind one of children, who, arms upraised, patiently wait for their parents to pick them up in a warm, loving, healing embrace.

Services began with three rousing group songs proclaiming and praising the love of Jesus. Then we all held hands. We held a group prayer. We were enjoined to pray to Jesūs Christ, healer of us all. We were told to pray to Jesus to not only heal us but to help heal others. We were called on to cleanse our bodies, to confess our sins, and to tell Jesus our fears, our jealousies, and our hates.

"Jesus cannot get into your bodies until you get rid of all that evil. That's what's making you sick — all of that bad in you, festering, sickening, growing like a cancer. You don't need it. Throw it out! Get rid of it! It's making you sick! It will kill you.!

"Tell Jesus. He'll forgive you. Jesus loves you. He understands. Tell Jesus your sins so that his forgiveness and his love can enter you. Let Jesus begin to heal you. Confession is good for you.

"Do you want to be healed?" he asked.

"Yes," shouted a variety of voices.

"Then get rid of all that filthy sin inside you. Let Jesus in. Healing begins with confession. Confession is good for the soul. Confession is good for the body. It's the beginning of healing.

"Confess!" exhorted the healer.

Persons were murmuring, confessing, crying. Some were alone. Others were with family or friends talking quietly, explaining, and listening. Some couples had their arms around each other. The front rows were filled with persons in wheelchairs and on crutches. Others were blind or deaf. Some were so weak they had to be supported.

"Now who's ready to be healed?" asked the healer.

"Come on up to me. Come on up here. If you really love Jesus, if you have really confessed your sins, you are ready. Jesus will heal you."

A line quickly began to form. It soon totalled over thirty persons. The first in line was an elderly man hobbling with the aid of two canes.

The healer asked him, "Do you believe in Jesus Christ? Do you believe that he can heal you? Have you confessed all of your sins? Have you let Jesus come in? Are you ready for Jesus to heal you?"

After receiving the appropriate assurances from the elderly gentleman, the healer asked, "Now then, what's wrong with you?"

The elderly gentleman replied that he had severe arthritis in his legs and joints, that he was always in pain, that he was getting worse, that he had been going to doctors for ten years and that they had been of little help.

The healer looked deep into the man's eyes and said, "If

you have faith, Jesus will heal you."

The healer then placed his hands around the elderly gentleman's forehead. He held them firmly, even tight, and begam to pray loudly: "Oh, Jesus, heal this sinner. Heal this sinner who has come back to you. Oh, Jesus, heal this sinner. Sweet Jesus, heal this man. Make his pains go away. Let him walk free again. Sweet Jesus, heal, heal. HEAL!"

He shouted this last word and gave the man a slight push. There was a gasp as the elderly man fell back into the arms of an attendant. The elderly man seemed dazed. He was laid out flat on the floor.

"Now stand up!" commanded the healer.

The man did that.

"You don't need these canes anymore, do you?"

The man slowly shook his head.

"Now show these people that you're healed. Walk over there. Come back here. That's right, Now do it fast. There you are."

The audience was clapping. Some were praying out loud: "Praise the Lord, praise the Lord."

"Now go over there and sit down," ordered the healer. He pointed to the front row near where I was sitting.

The man walked over to sit down three seats from me. He walked rather slowly and stiffly. He seemed uncertain or afraid or still dazed. He sat there in silence.

A middle-aged woman was now being led up to the healer. Again the questions, again the assurances. Her complaint to him was that she was going blind. She could now only see shadows and even that was dimming. Again the healer's prayers and calls to Jesus, and then he suddenly clapped her across her eyes. She fell back into the arms of the waiting helper. She too was laid out on the floor.

After a moment of rather dramatic wait, the healer said, "Now let us help her up."

This was done and he commanded the lady, "Open your eyes. Jesus wants you to see better. Can you see better?"

She nodded.

"How many hands am I holding up?" He held up his right hand. "One," she replied. "How many fingers am I holding up?" He raised his thumb. "One," she replied.

The lady began to cry.

"Now go over there and sit down," he commanded. She came over and sat down next to the man.

The healing process went on; a number of persons walking with the aid of canes or crutches, some with difficulty in seeing, others hard-of-hearing, those with aching pains, some with skin disorders, a few cancer cases, and one young man with leukemia. All of these persons claimed, in some degree or another, to "feel better," to "be better," to have "no pain," to have felt "Jesus touched me," or to feel "healed."

# TWO FOR THE PRICE OF ONE

A N uncommon scene from the usual range of healing services took place in Tampa, Florida.

The service was held in an old home, the three-story type built of solid lumber. A long porch ran the front width of the house. The first floor held a large living room and a large dining room, both off the entrance hall, and a number of other rooms. The second floor contained a small library and classrooms. The third floor was private for the family of the healer. We met on the first floor in the living room with the sliding doors to the dining room open. Both rooms were thus available.

There were some forty persons already seated when I came in. The healer was playing an organ. Up front, before the audience, were four stools. Behind each stool was a healer or student of healing. One by one, members of the audience came up to be healed. Each of us waited our turn and then went up to sit down. Behind us, the healer passed her hands over our heads, down our bodies, and along our sides. The healer then rubbed our backs and stroked our shoulders. The entire process took only some five minutes. While there may have been therapeutic side effects, the main purpose of the exercise seemed to be that of uniting the audience into feeling they were a common group, united for a common goal, for a common good. Individuals were relaxed and smiling after the exchange.

After all the audience members had been up to be "healed," the healing service was closed. Then the healers began to practice clairvoyance.

"May I contact you?" The healer asked an old man in the audience.

He nodded eagerly.

"You are very unhappy. You feel overwhelmed by your troubles. Do not despair. Jesus is on your side. He is waiting to help you. Have you prayed to Jesus, asking him to help you? Do that tonight. I see your troubles going away. It's about your children, is it not? Yes, your children have been worrying you. But do not worry. Your children will soon resolve their problems. It will work out."

The next healer turned to a young lady.

"May I contact you?"

Again the eager nod.

"You are thinking about your work. Yes, the job may be getting you down. I see you making a move. You have been considering a move. Yes, it is all right. You will be better for it."

And so the healers went on, asking if they could contact the individual. No one refused. And then they went on to "see" their personal problems and predict their paths of resolution. The purchase of a new car was recommended, a projected long trip was decided, familial crises advised, and engagements and marriages encouraged. As I recall, I was given some kind words about my career.

A small box was then passed around and virtually everyone put in their dollar bill. It seemed to be considered money well invested. Healing and clairvoyance, two for the price of one.

Everyone left with a positive glow. We were all encouraged, comforted. We were all given "answers."

# BATTELL CHAPEL HEALING

A most unusual healing service was held at the Yale University Battell Chapel. It was a rather fresh evening; there was a chilly rain falling. An overcast, cloudy sky made the darkness come in early and pronouncedly. Despite all of this gloom, the chapel was absolutely full. Some persons were standing in the back and along the side aisles.

This healing service was led by a team of attractive young men and women. They led us in spirited singing and praying. Handclapping and swaying accompanied the music and chanting. There were some brief religious exhortations concerning love and forgiveness and mercy and healing. There were promises of good health and healing miracles. The atmosphere in the room was one of happiness, joy, and festivity. Even the obviously sick and suffering seemed to be in good spirits.

Then the healer was called on. She was a young woman, perhaps in her early thirties with rich hair, a full body, and a form-fitting dress. She was attractive; she made a striking appearance and she knew it. She strode confidently among the audience.

"Jesus loves you," she declared, "I love you."

"I know that you have troubles. I know that you are tired and upset. Life has too many problems, too many decisions. I understand, and I want to help you. I love you — all of you. I love you because Jesus loves you. The love of Jesus fills my body. I am overflowing with love for you. Jesus loves you. Jesus wants to heal you. Love, love, love is the way to be healed."

"Oh, Jesus," she prayed, "help me heal these poor sinners. Oh, Jesus, give me the power to heal these unfortunate sinners."

She paused, looked around at us, "Are you ready to be healed?" she asked.

"Yes, yes," came a variety of voices.

She closed her eyes and held out her hands. There was a tense silence.

"There's a lung out there," she announced, "It has just been healed. Stand up. Where is that healthy lung. You've just been healed."

After a moment, an elderly gentleman stood up.

"Come on up here to the platform" she ordered.

"Now it is a knee that's been healed. A knee has been healed. Stand up. Show us who you are. Come up here."

A middle-aged woman stood up and began to walk up to the platform.

The proclaimed healings went on: a "lower lip and a jaw," a "stomach ulcer," "difficult hearing," and "a troubled heart."

Soon there were some twenty persons up on the stage waiting to testify that they had been healed of specific ailments.

# JESUS THE HEALER

THESE references to Jesus as the master of all healing — the Healer — have their roots in the New Testament. Tillich (1967) argues that the ideal *soter* (savior) of that period in Judaism was the healer "who makes healthy and whole." According to Tillich, the New Testament accounts of healing should not be taken as stories of miracles but rather as stories demonstrating Jesus as the True Savior, as the Universal Healer. Jesus was the Christ by virtue of his demonstrated healings.

The Gospels emphasize these healing powers of Jesus: "And wherever he came, in villages, cities, or country, they laid the sick in the market places, and besought Him that they might touch even the fringe of his garment; and as many touched it were made well" (Mark 6:56).

There are some theologians who state that the healings of Jesus are really allegories of great religious import. For example, following this reasoning, when Jesus healed the two blind men at Jericho, the real meaning of the healing is as follows: Jericho is the world, the two blind men are Israel and Judea, and Jesus has given them Light to see the New Message.

Whatever the merits of the reasoning, the fact remains that Christianity is unique among the world religions in that it places healing as such a central religious theme, an integral factor in its theology, and an essential part of its practice. All of this is due, certainly, to the Gospel reports of the

41

healings by Jesus.

There are any number of collections of the healing miracles of Jesus, and Hereward Carrington (1935, pp. 48-51) has published one useful classification. Despite the brevity of the mission of Jesus, the number of his specific miracles reported in the New Testament total some thirty-five, twenty-six of which relate to healing in one form or another.

Specifically they relate to:

| | |
|---|---|
| The cure of lepers | Two cases |
| The curing of blind and dumb | Five cases |
| The exorcising of demons | Six cases |
| The raising of dead | Three cases |
| Miscellaneous healings | Ten cases |

The specific references are:

The healing of the leper (Matt. 8:2-4, Mark 1:40-45, Luke 5: 12-16).

The healing of Peter's mother-in-law (Matt. 8:14-15, Mark 1: 29-31, Luke 4:38-39).

The healing of the paralytic (Matt. 9:28, Mark 2:1-12, Luke 5: 18-26).

The healing of the withered hand (Matt. 12:9-14, Mark 3:1-6, Luke 6:6-11).

The demoniac of Gadara (Matt. 8:28-34, Mark 5:1-20, Luke 8: 26-39).

The woman with an issue of blood (Matt. 9:20-22, Mark 5:25-34, Luke 8:43-48).

The raising of the daughter of Jarius (Matt. 9:18-19, 23-26, Mark 5:22-24. 35-43. Luke 8:41-42, 49-56).

The healing of the lunatic boy (Matt. 17:14-21, Mark 9:14-29, Luke 9:37-43).

The healing of the blind men at Jericho (Matt. 20:29-34, Mark 10: 46-52, Luke 18:35-43).

The healing of the daughter of the Canaanite Woman (Matt. 15: 21-28, Mark 7:24-30).

The healing of the servant of the Centurion (Matt. 8:5-13. Luke 7: 1-10).

The healing of the dumb demoniac (Matt. 9:32-33, Luke 11:14).

The healing of a demoniac in the Capernaum synagogue (Mark 1:23-26, Luke 4:33-36).

The healing of two blind men (Matt. 9:29-31).

The healing of a demoniac (Matt. 12:22).

The healing of one deaf and dumb (Mark 7:31-37).

The opening of the eyes of one blind at Bethsaida (Mark 9:22-26).

The raising of the widow's son (Luke 7:11-17).

The curing of the woman with the spirit of infirmity (Luke 13:10-17).

The curing of the dropsied man (Luke 14:1-6).

The cleansing of the ten lepers (Luke 17:12-19).

The healing of the ear of Malchus (Luke 22:49-51).

The healing of the son of the nobleman (John 4:46-54).

The healing of the impotent man at Bethesda (John 5:1-16).

The opening of the eyes of one born blind (John 9).

The raising of Lazarus (John 11:1-54).

# THE WORLD'S OLDEST PROFESSION

RELIGION and healing, of course, have a long and complex history of intimate relationships. Around the world, across time and space, the study of virtually every culture reveals the important role of healing among the responsibilities of the religion.

Religious leaders are frequently also the medical leaders. The very terms "medicine man," "shaman," "witch doctor," and "faith healer" are merely some examples of the recognition of the potential oneness of this role. Contrary to popular opinion, the world's oldest profession may actually be that of the healers.

The Middle East has an early and lengthy documented relationship between religion and healing. Gudea, the Sumerian, and Hammurabi, the Babylonian, are two examples of second and first millenium B.C. Mesopotamian priest-kings who are credited with possessing powers to invoke sickness, pain, and death, as well as possessing powers to heal the victims of such suffering.

By the time of the *Odyssey*, Pharonic Egyptian priests were famous for their medical expertise. Similar to the Mesopotamians, the medical system of the Egyptians incorporated nonreligious material, e.g. The Ebers Papyrus, along with a variety of traditional religious beliefs and practices.

This complex medical interaction was manifested also among the early Greeks. By the fifth century B.C. they were practicing both the reasonings of the schools of Hippocrates as well as Aesclepios. Both of these schools may be traced back to earlier Egyptian and Mesopotamian influences.

The Old Testament indicates that health and disease were considered manifestations of divine power. Healing was in the hands of God ("I am the Lord that healeth thee." Ex.15:26). The healers (*ro-phim*) were essentially the helpers, or instruments, of God. The Hebrew priesthood was responsible for enforcing the Biblical injunctions pertaining to social hygiene and public health. Of the 613 commandments in the Old Testament, 213 are of a medical nature. Hygiene and prophylaxis were religious dogma to protect the public health of the entire community.

By the time of Jesus, a sect of Jewish religious purists, called the Essenes, were also known for their reputed medical knowledge. One of the interpretations given to their name is that of *a-si-im* or "healers." Centered apparently at Qumran, along the Dead Sea, they were a significant religious community during the time of John the Baptist, Jesus, and Paul. Qumran was destroyed sometime around the year 70, after the Romans burned the Temple in Jerusalem.

Jesus, then, as a religious healer, was part of a profound Middle Eastern tradition. Jesus was understood, accepted, and revered within these terms of reference. No other religous leader, however, made healing so central a theme in his ministry; no other religion has made healing so major a concern within its practice. This is a unique phenomenon.

# THE MYSTIC AND THE MEDIC

WE are all aware of the seemingly intimate relationship between religion and medicine. Physicians and clergy are often called upon to help treat the same fear, pain, anguish, and suffering. Moments of dying and death are occasions for both professions to operate together simultaneously.

Medicine may well be rooted in a religious heritage. The "witch doctor," "shaman," "medicine man," and "healer" are merely some of the terms that acknowledge this professional relationship. Physicians have long recognized this. At least one authoritative medical body, the Group for the Advancement of Psychiatry (1960), has called for the serious study of religion in order to learn how to better utilize it in understanding and treating the mentally ill.

E. Fuller Torrey argues that witch doctors and psychiatrists, however they are both defined, practice essentially similar processes of therapy that result in not dissimilar rates of "healing."

John White, Professor of Psychiatry at the University of Manitoba, advocates praying as a therapeutic force (1977). Prayer, says White, may be essential to religion, but it can also operate positively to help cope with illness. Prayer, he advances, can help to initiate the healing process.

White cites, updates, and amplifies the oft-quoted statement of Alexis Carrel: "As a physician I have seen men, after all other therapy has failed, lifted out of disease and melan-

46

choly by the serene effort of prayer.")

Allen R. Andrews has called for more psychologists to study "the religious dimensions of human experience" (1979, p. 37).

We need to understand these phenomena in a far more objective and comprehensive manner. We need to better understand, for example, the work of Anton Boisen.

Anton Boisen was both a psychologist of religion and a schizophrenic. He had to be hospitalized for a number of psychotic episodes. Boisen, however, has an important and well-deserved place in the psychology of religion. He was largely responsible for establishing clinical training in counseling for clergy. Boisen, as Jung, was able to use experiences drawn from personal psychotic episodes to help formulate and develop psychological theories and teachings. (For a fuller discussion of this subject, see "Anton Boisen Revisited" by Lucy Bregman, *Journal of Religion and Health*, July 1979, pp. 213-229.)

Viktor Frankl, survivor of Auschwitz, has developed his theory of "logotherapy" as a potential bridge between religion and psychotherapy. Frankl says that patients sometimes complain of an inner void or emptiness. These patients are, he says, witnesses to a complete futility of life. They are a negation of any value to life. They suffer from an "existential vacuum" (1967, p. 177). They will not survive. "Men are strong [only] as long as they represent a strong idea," argues Frankl (1967, p. 185).

Philosophers may also provide useful insights. Martin Buber advocated an "I-Thou" intimacy with God: an "uninhibited and total mutuality" between God and person.

Religion and medicine, the mystic and the medic, may have a long heritage but it is still too little understood. Many persons believe that religion, a faith in God, is essential to human well-being and survival.

Is mysticism an essential part of this? Do we, as humans, have an absolute need for transient episodes of profound emotional experiences?

Mystics argue that spiritual ecstasy is a necessary human experience. Faith healers seem to call on this fervor to help establish the healing process.

Such emotional experiences may also have pragmatic, political consequences. We recall the Great Awakening, that widespread, intensely personal and emotional religious revival that swept across the northeastern seaboard of America in the early 1700s.

There were many American and British religious leaders who mistrusted these emotional scenes. Jonathan Edwards, widely respected for his academic scholarship and religious rationalism, viewed, studied, and analyzed the Great Awakening. He came out as one of its staunch supporters and defenders. Richard Hutch (1968) argues that Jonathan Edwards helped provide religious respectability for American revivalism and, by extension, helped make healing services a legitimate part of the religious service.

Precipitating, and perhaps part of, the Great Awakening was the fact that New England had only recently been swept by a series of epidemic diseases. One serious epidemic, called "the throat distemper," was actually three separate epidemics — one of scarlet fever and two of diptheria — that killed over 5,000 persons, mostly children and young people, within a cold five-year period. The tragedies were regarded as Acts of God (Vaux, 1978, pp. 14-15).

Whatever the cause, another of the more significant results of the Great Awakening was that it greatly stimulated and helped develop a pronounced social and political unity among the thirteen colonies. This was on the eve of the Revolutionary War. United States' independence may owe not a small debt of gratitude to those eighteenth century faith healers working among America's coastal and frontier populations.

The mystic and the medic may be better comprehended if we can begin to realize a fundamental issue. You are not necessarily a body with a mind. You are much more a mind located in a body. The mind is the essence of your humanity;

without it you are as the other animals. It is our mind that makes us unique.

Mind, spirit, soul — whatever you wish to call it — that is the reality of our living. It is our life force, our *élan vital*. The body is the expression of the mind. Faith healing, correctly, focuses on the mind as the primary issue for healing. It is the mystic and the mystical experience that may make the medic.

# A PROPOSED PARADIGM

A T this juncture, it is important that we pause and consider. It is appropriate to try to step back from this mass of descriptive material.

I suggest that we need a theoretical model, a paradigm, to begin to structure all of this data. We need to begin to sort it out. We need to try and make sense of it all. I suggest that one can discern here a pattern. There is a logical process at work. This proposed paradigm is, at best, a tentative, generalized model. It is proposed to help us understand the dynamics of faith healing services.

These are, as it were, a set of guidelines. Obviously, you do not necessarily need to follow all of these guidelines in order to arrive at a successful healing. Furthermore, and unfortunately, following all of these guidelines will not necessarily guarantee a successful healing. These guidelines are a distillation of my thirty years of field investigations. They are a summary of over a quarter century of experiences.

I have seen these work. I cannot guarantee that they will work in every instance or for every supplicant. In my experience, not all faith healing is exaggerated, and not all faith healers are charlatans. The religious experience can be a therapeutic process.

Consider these reasonings. Test them; improve on them.

# THE RIGHT SETTING

IN order to maximize the effectiveness of the healing service, it should be conducted in an appropriate setting.

A religious atmosphere is important, although not essential. A church, cathedral, temple, monastery, or retreat are obvious supportive settings. A cave or spring with a religious tradition or a particular home that has achieved a holy aura, is helpful to the establishment of an atmosphere of sanctity.

In certain instances the walls of the healing room may be covered with glowing testimonials from healed patients. Photographs may dramatize the events. There may even be, particularly among illiterate populations, discarded crutches and supports, and patches and bandages. These are no longer needed by the healed. Even models of healed limps and organs may be displayed. These are all "proof positive" of the healing success of this locale. All of this, of course, serves to heighten and reinforce the expectations of the patients and their families.

"If so many persons have been healed of all of these ailments," reasons the patient, "then surely I also can be healed."

This expectation is heightened even further if the patient must travel a long distance to the healing setting: preparations involve the entire family; expenses are incurred; shopping is necessary; maps are studied; travel agents are consulted; travel itself is exciting; boredom and monotony are replaced with excitement and change; hopes are raised; and expectations are elevated. The longer the distance, the harder the road, and the more enduring the suffering — these only serve to build up the feelings. By the time that the patients arrive at the setting, their emotions are at fever pitch.

(It is said that the most emotional scenes at Lourdes are not at the cave, where the healings are hoped for, but at the train station when the suffering arrive and disembark. It is also said, for this reason, that no one from Lourdes is ever healed at Lourdes.)

Pilgrimages, of themselves, can be therapeutic. It is as if the long and arduous journey, replete with visible suffering and uncomplaining endurance, serves to justify the healing. Sometimes the patients, or members of their families, will fast; they will go without food and drink. Others will crawl on their hands and knees through the last stage of the pilgrimage. Some will stand throughout the long healing service. Such visible suffering can only soften the heart of God. Surely God cannot refuse to help such persons, whatever their sins.

# A "CLOUD OF WITNESSES"

THE healing ceremony itself is conducted in the midst of a cloud of witnesses: a host of patients, families, friends, well-wishers, and curious spectators, ideally all of them confined within the healing hall. The healer stands before them; the manifestly supportive families surround them. The walls are covered with proofs of the healer's successes. The atmosphere in the room is charged with excitement. The mass of people are gripped with emotion. They are singing, chanting, praying, praising, and crying. The very air is electric with tension.

All of this reacts directly and profoundly on the patients. So many persons are visibly on their side, rooting for them, and wanting the healing to succeed. The healing has got to work; it will work. The patient cannot disappoint so many persons. It is the self-fulfilling prophecy working positively. The patient wants the healing to succeed. Therefore, to one degree or another, the healing will succeed.

The cloud of witnesses provides support to the patient in this moment of trial. The cloud of witnesses expects a healing to occur by virtue of their massed attendance. It is a tense, fever-pitched scene. Many in the crowd are standing, arms upraised. Some have wrapped themselves around the patients; others are holding onto them; encouraging them, lavishing love, and expectation.

In such an emotion-charged atmosphere, the patient dare not disappoint the host. The patient must be healed.

Hebrews 12 lives!

# THE GREAT HEALER

CROSS-CULTURALLY — I mean by that whether I was working among American Indians, North Chinese farmers, South Vietnamese city folk, Christian Arab villagers, Muslim Nigerian traders, or middle-class Americans in the megalopolis — one factor is constant: the faith healers are invariably cast from the same mold.

The ideal faith healer is a Mother or Father figure: strong, firm, merciful, understanding, loving, stern, supportive, commanding, and compassionate. All of these terms are not contradictory. On the contrary, they are the collection of images that we project onto our healer. He or she is all of these characteristics. Thus we can draw on any of them as we need them.

First and foremost your healer truly, truly cares about you. Your healer truly, truly loves you. He understands you and he wants to help you. Your healer has the power to help you; he has the power to heal you. Your suffering has not gone unnoticed. Your endurance will be rewarded.

Gaze upon the face of the healer and expect only good things to flow to you from that inexhaustible source of strength. First, however, you must fulfill your responsibilities.

# YOU – THE HEALEE

YOU must begin by answering a painful question: "Do you really want to get well?"

Despite everything that has been said thus far, it cannot be assumed that the obviously suffering patient necessarily really does want to be healed. The desire to be healed is not always a given.

Illness can be a very useful crutch to help you resolve your other life problems. A difficult boss, an uncaring husband, or ungrateful children can be made to feel sorry for you if you are ill.

"Who said I'm a failure? It is not true."

"I was doing fine until I started to get 'these terrible headaches,' 'this nagging backache,' 'the sudden heart attack,' or 'this painful cancer.'" The more obvious the suffering, the more legitimate the illness. You no longer need to prove yourself; you no longer need to justify yourself; you no longer need to strive; you are ill.

The anger and resentment of others toward you, their scorn and their sarcasm no longer exist. Your illness makes them convert it to sympathy and understanding. You might still be dismissed from your job, but now it is for a legitimate reason. There is no cause for conflict because face has been saved for both sides.

# YOUR PUBLIC CONFESSION

O NE of the most effective methods of dredging up the materials related to the honest answering of the question, "Do you really want to get well?" is through the process of public confession.

Mark Twain once said that we are the only animal that can blush, or needs to.

We human beings, apparently, are the only animal that feels the need to confess. Most of us, apparently, are capable of greed, gossip, envy, jealousy, lying, lust, treachery, even torture and murder, as well as a host of other unpleasant traits. We recognize that many of us, apparently, are guilty at different times of practicing some of these traits. We understand that a few of us find the burden of these sins too much to bear. Our guilt overwhelms us; our sins weigh us down. The burden is too much; it is making us sick.

Public confession is a human way of throwing off this burden of guilt and washing away one's sins. Public confession is a form of public penance and public abasement.

You demonstrate that you truly want to be healed by publicly confessing your load of sins. The healer and the cloud of witnesses hear you: we understand you; we forgive you. You are ready to be healed. You have paid public penance. You have earned the right to be healed.

You are ready, eager, and impatient!

# THE HEALING

THE healer is now ready to initiate the healing process. It generally proceeds along three stages.

First, the healer pronounces a positive prognosis: "You will get well! I can heal you!"

These are powerful pronouncements, and the audience and the patients know that only good healing can flow from such strength.

Next, the healer initiates his actual healing on the patient. The patient will be touched, held, stroked or massaged. Holy water or holy oil might be rubbed onto the painful body. The cross of Jesus may be given to the patient to grasp, to hold to the forehead, or over the heart.

While all of this is going on, the healer might pray loudly: "Sweet Jesus, help this poor sinner. Heal her, sweet Jesus. She has paid for her sins. Oh, Jesus, this Christian needs your help. Heal her, Jesus, heal her."

Then the healer will turn to the patient and shout the commandment: "You are healed!" "Stand up straight." "Throw away your crutch!" "Open your eyes!" "Lift up your arms!"

In an interesting number of cases, that is precisely what the patients do. They obey the commandment. They claim to be healed. They claim that they "feel better," that the pain is "gone," that they can "see," "hear," "walk," or "talk." They claim that they have been "healed."

For how many persons this is a real healing, a lasting healing, or a permanent healing — we do not know.

At Lourdes, we recall, despite the fact that the French Academy of Medicine has recognized only fifty-four real miracles of healing, millions of patients continue to claim that they were healed there, or felt better, or had temporary relief from pain and suffering. Patients who were helpless and hopeless, or depressed, despondent, demoralized, defeated, and dying claim to have been rejuvenated, transformed, or reborn. This, too, can be a healing.

# TELESCOPED TIME THERAPY

I suggest that the faith healing that may take place is really a manifestation of telescoped time therapy.

Faith healing is a radically speeded-up version of the potential normal healing process. Suppurating sores dry up and new skin grows over; ulcers close up. Muscular constrictions ease off; crippled limbs straighten out. Wildly spreading cancer cells become controlled, curtailed, or killed. Agonizing heart pains cease as coronary constrictions ease up. Ear inflammations and eye films clear up. Internal organs such as the liver, kidneys, gall bladder, or sexual organs seem to take control of themselves in a positive, therapeutic manner.

The "miracle" of healing, I say, is the sudden acceleration of potential, normative healing processes. Flesh burns and lacerations begin to close over with new skin. Muscles cease their painful contractions. Bone stiffness seems to become oiled and soothed. Internal organs return to their normal quiescent functioning. Acute pain seems to be made more bearable. Dull and throbbing pain seems to recede. The senses seem to be revitalized. Vision, hearing, taste, and smell seem to improve. The person seems to be rejuvenated: the back straightens up, the head is held erect, the eyes sparkle, and the skin glows. Grim facial lines seem less furrowed and less foreboding. It is a miracle!

Of course, not all of this complex of positive physical improvement happens to every person attending the faith healing service. This is merely some of the range of physical benefits that may result. Faith healing, in other words, does not necessarily need to be explained in terms of magic or miracles.

What never occurs is the sudden bursting out of a shock of hair on a previously bald head or the sudden appearance of a new limb where one had previously been amputated or missing from birth. These would be real miracles.

My experience has been that the faith healing services are miracles in the sense that the regenerative healing forces within the body are suddenly and rapidly generated in a manner far superior to the normal range of expectation.

What does happen is that the potential healing processes, which could be expected to require a long period of time, with slow but gradual healing, suddenly, rapidly, and seemingly spontaneously begin to effect almost instantaneous healing. Faith healing absolutely telescopes the healing period. Instead of years, months, or weeks, the healing takes moments.

That is the miracle: the fact is that the mind can heal the body, and incredibly quickly. Faith healing, when it works, is telescoped time therapy.

# "WHAT DO I HAVE TO LIVE FOR?"

EVERY suffering person with a painful, crippling, or killing sickness must ask an important question. "What do I have to live for?" Slowly think through an honest answer.

The patient must ask this question. The sufferer must think through the answer; then write it down, study it, and revise it. The sick should keep it somewhere before them, "as frontlets before their eyes."

The more full, satisfying, and growing the reply, the more speedy the potential recovery.

You, the patient, must ask this question of yourself. If you can only reply negatively, that you have nothing to live for, then the more serious your illness, the more the pain, and the more you will suffer. You must have a reason to get well; you must have something to live for. You must want to live. You must be able to answer this question honestly and positively. If not, you almost certainly will not be healed.

# THE ETHICAL CONTRACT

OBVIOUS questions come to mind: "What type of persons are most likely to be healed?" "What can I do to help ensure that I will be healed?" "What can we do to help our loved one be healed?"

Obviously, no one can yet state categorical answers to such fundamental questions. I shall here structure a certain process of reasoning. Hopefully, this will provide a degree of understanding and insight into the nature and complexity of these questions and their resolution.

The basis of this reasoning is that illness and pain, and sickenss and suffering are the result of sin. Sin causes suffering.

Jealousy, envy, greed, abuse of power, resentment, anger, and hatred will make you, the sinner, sick. You will suffer until you confess your sins. You will suffer until you rid yourself of these sins. Then, and only then, can Jesus Christ come in and heal you.

I have found it useful to consider certain reasoning of James E. Dittes. In his seminal work, *Bias and the Pious* (in particular Chapter 4, "Prodigal Faith and Contractual Faith," pp. 65-81), Dittes takes Luke's recording of the parable of the prodigal son (Luke 15:11-32) and proposes an exegesis: One can postulate two different styles of life and faith — two understandings of how God relates to a person and how a person is to relate to God and his fellow person. Dittes calls these two styles contractual and prodigal.

62

The contractual religious approach is for the person to do good works and to be rewarded by God accordingly. The prodigal religious approach is to open oneself "with abandon and without reserve to receive the unreserved and undeserved grace of God" (pp. 68-69). "The difference," says Dittes, "is the difference between an emphasis on our *doing* and on our *being*."(emphasis added).

Obviously, good works are important, he goes on, but the peril is to construct of them a contract with God and then rely on them. Salvation does not depend on good works. Dittes cites Paul and Luther who have taught that elements of work and the law have legitimate but subordinate places in religion. The prodigal life of grace and faith is above and beyond.

I suggest that this reasoning has relevance to the dynamics of faith healing services. I suggest that persons most amenable to faith healing are those who have, as it were, made a contract with God: for good works rendered, for loyalty, devotion, obedience, and faithful service, God will reward his servant. The contract will be honored; the demonstrated good behavior will be recognized.

Obviously it is important to have faith in order to expect God's grace, but apparently it is considered to be a bit much to expect God's healing to be entirely unearned. In this case, faith is important and essential, but it is not enough. Faith must be accompanied by good works.

(Good works can also be interpreted as public confession − honest, painful, heart-wrenching, and public promise − to henceforth live the good life and do good works.)

This reasoning has a pronounced religious tradition. Refer, for example, to the argument of Edward Schillebeeckx (1979, especially pp. 179-200). For additional perspective it might be useful to begin with the small *Festschrift* to Edward Schillebeeckx for his sixtieth birthday (Huizing and Bassett, 1974), with particular reference to "Confirmation as the Completing of Baptism" by Hans Kung (pp. 79-99).

One is reminded of the poem by John Donne, the former Dean of St. Paul's Church, to the effect that man is his "own executioner." Dietrich Bonhoeffer, that minister who did not keep silent during the Holocaust, once summarized this theological argument very effectively: "Cheap grace is the preaching of forgiveness without requiring repentance" (1959, p. 36). Over 1500 years ago Tertullian wrote, "How absurd it is to leave the penance unperformed, and yet expect forgiveness of sins" (Aulen, 1937, p. 97).

There is a strong religious tradition justifying the contractual model. God will heal those who have honored their contract; they must pay for their sins.

In the faith healing services that I studied, the contractual model of this theology seems to be most operative. The participants, both the healers and those hoping to be healed, are very familiar with Christian prayers, songs, and normative religious behavior acceptable to Jesus Christ. They recognize, or are prepared to recognize, that they have erred in their relationship with God. They have sinned; they have violated the contract. Illness, pain, and suffering are the explicit results. Now they are ready to atone. They are prepared, even eager, after the appropriate public emotion and support, to make public confession and public penance. They want to confess their sins, the errors of their ways, and their transgressions. The burden is too heavy to bear. These sinners want to unload themselves of their burdens of guilt, remorse, and shame.

Public confession is not forced on them. On the contrary, they do it voluntarily. It feels so good, physically as well as emotionally, to unload the burden and to cleanse oneself of one's sins. It is such a relief to finally admit, to shout out, one's small-minded jealousies, petty greed, or mean actions. Now they can begin to reestablish that right relationship with God. Public confession will be followed by public penance. Henceforth, vow the past sinners, they will lead the good Christian life. Faith, hope, and charity will be the foundation stones of their new lives.

The emphasis in this vowed public penance is on living the good Christian life. They will abstain from sin and disavow evil; they swear to do good works. They will reward this faith healer for his religious deeds. Public confession and vowed public penance, if truly honest and sincere, will lead to God's merciful forgiveness. There will be a public healing; the punishment of pain and suffering will be lifted. The public healing will be demonstrable proof of God's merciful forgiveness; God has accepted the public confession and public penance and has bestowed public healing.

Jesus Christ is the medium for all of this to be activated and effected: only through Jesus Christ can the contract between sinner and God be reestablished; only through Jesus Christ will the contract be maintained; only through Jesus Christ do the Old and New Testaments unite and make God's purpose manifest.

Persons coming to a faith healer expect no simple miracles. They realize that they are responsible to some degree for their own ill-health, pain, and suffering. They acknowledge that they have violated their contract with God; they recognize that God has punished them accordingly. In order to be healed, they must reestablish their contract with God. That is the purpose of the faith healing service. It is to help them reestablish that right relationship with God. By illness, their credibility has been questioned; their performance has been found wanting. Now they have come to restore the right relationship. They want to reestablish the contract.

In good faith they confess their sins. In good faith they vow penance. In good faith they expect to be healed. The degree of their honesty and sincerity, as manifested in public confession and public penance, will determine the degree of their public healing.

No one of these persons expects God to just heal them. No one expects God to reestablish the contract without any fundamental changes on their part. That would violate the meaning and weaken the efficacy of an honest contractual relationship.

The working model of the prodigal relationship, I suggest, is not so much beyond their ken as it is just not appropriate or rational. The prodigal relationship is too one-sided. God's love may be poured out on them, "unreserved and undeserved," even while they remain sinful, continue to practice evil, and blatantly violate the contract.

This makes for uneasiness. The very uncontrolled aspect of it is frightening. It is too unpredictable. If God can pour out his love in so unreserved a fashion, even while one is sinful, God might just as unreservedly withdraw that love.

A contract, however, is much more secure. The contract is much more predictable. It is binding between God and person. A contract between God and person, established and honored in good faith, can only lead to God's blessings of good health. Accordingly, if the sick person will henceforth honor the contract, God will honor the contract. Full and honest confession and sincere repentance will lead to healing. Henceforth, living the good Christian life will ensure that the contract of good health will also be so honored.

Based upon my research, I believe that those persons most devoutly attending healing services, those persons most successfully healed, are of the contractual religious type. I suggest that their personalities; their life experiences; and their religious knowledge, activities, expectations and fervor differ profoundly and significantly from, at least, the prodigal religious type. Further, I suggest that a careful study of faith healers will reveal that they exemplify, *par excellence,* the contractual religious type. Such faith healers, certainly the most successful of them, find the contractual religious model to be most congenial for them within which to operate.

It makes their role as a faith healer most logical, most coherent, and most legitimate. They are among the "cloud of witnesses" helping the sinners, the punished, and the suffering to find their way back to God. They are helping them turn away from evil. They will cease sinning, and they will thus be healed. The faith healer is helping to effect all of this goodness. Under these terms of reference, the faith healer can  truly be seen as a servant of God. The faith healer is truly fulfilling an honorable task for God. Any rewards that the faith healer receives, the faith healer has earned honestly and fairly. Such earthly rewards, anyway, are as nothing compared with the rewards to be received from Jesus Christ in Heaven.

Money collecting, of course, is an integral part of these faith healing services. At the Yale healing, large white plastic buckets were passed from hand to hand. In Tampa, each of us was handed a contribution envelope as we walked into the room. These were collected after the singing and praying but before the actual healings began. Faith healing services require quite a staff of musicians, singers, group leaders, ushers, and usherettes, all in addition to the actual faith healer. The willingness to contribute money by the hoped-to-be healed and their families, as a public demonstration of faith and good works, is an undeniable factor of importance. Faith healing is not an insignificant financial undertaking — either for faith healers or those hoping to be healed.

Faith healing, let us be clear, is not all fraud. Faith healers are not all charlatans. The ethical contract is a religious bond between God and person. If given in good faith, it can and will be honored.

This helps to explain a curious phenomena that may sometimes be seen at faith healing services. Obviously, the devout religious believer is a natural potential for faith healing but, interestingly, antagonistic, agnostic children of profoundly religious parents may undergo emotional-charged miraculous changes at faith healing services.

I suggest that children with highly emotional rejections of their parents, consciously or unconsciously, may find compatible such a religious scene to make their dramatic return to their parents, family friends, religion, and their entire social way of life. It is a heart-warming moment, splendid in its drama, as the prodigal son returns to the bosom of the family. The ethical contract has been demonstrated again.

(Another perspective of this prodigal versus contractual dichotomy may be found in the paper "Covenant versus Con-

tract as Two Modes of Relationship Orientation: On Recon-
ciling Possibility and Necessity," by Kalman J. Kaplan and
Moriah Markus-Kaplan, 1979.)

# "MY EYES! MY EYES!"

SINCE the pioneering work of Freud and his classic exposition of the Oedipus complex, psychoanalysts have recognized the powerful emotional relationship between the male reproductive organs and the eyes.

Oedipus, we recall, stabbed out his eyes when he learned that he had murdered his father and married his mother. Sophocles related the scene most dramatically:

> Not once, but many times,
> He raised his hands and stabbed his eyes;
> So that from both of them the blood ran down his face,
> Not drop by drop, but all at once,
> In a dark flow of gore. (Young, 1906, p. 166)

Psychoanalysts today, however, are finding another manifestation of this genital-visual relationship. Some men, as they move into their midforties, develop aggravated fears of loss of manhood, e.g. the inability to achieve or maintain an erection. This fear of sexual impotence can be so powerful and pervasive that eye problems seem to be a resultant concomitant. Among such men, there may develop a worsening of the visual faculty, difficulties in focusing, sudden eye strain, blinding headaches, and even detached retinas.

Although there is much to be explored here, it seems to be emerging that today, as in the days of the ancient Greeks, male sexual behavior and eye problems may not have an unimportant relationship. Healing visual problems for middle-aged men at the faith healing services may have deeper heal-

ing concomitants. Feared male impotency may be the un-
stated hoped-for healing.

# THE FEMALE OF THE SPECIES

DURING my research into faith healing, I am constantly impressed with the audiences: these self-selected populations of voluntarily attending persons. Such persons are mainly, if not solely, over the age of forty.

Children, teenagers, and young adults in their twenties and thirties are rarely found at a faith healing service. On the occasional times that they are in attendance, it is for unusual circumstances: a child with birth defects, a teenager suffering from leukemia, or a young girl crippled in an accident. Young people, unfortunately, as I noted earlier, die primarily from accidents, homicides, and suicides. A few die from infectious diseases. A very few die from degenerative diseases such as cancer or stroke. They do not suffer, generally, from the chronic ailments and disabilities afflicting the middle-aged and the elderly.

In my experience, it is the forty-and-over group that constitutes the majority of the audiences at faith healing services. Faith healing services are directed to them. It is this age group that needs faith healings; it is this age group that supports faith healing services. As our population continues in its general aging direction, incidentally, we may expect then that faith healers and faith healing services will continue to grow in popularity.

As we move into our forties, then, we approach the danger zone. Negative mind-over-body control can become more manifest, more pervasive, and more dangerous. It is relevant to recognize a unique physiological phenomenon of this age group. I refer, of course, to menopause.

We are familiar with the mass of material that has been written about the menopausal female and her physiological changes, emotional problems, and social adjustments. Even while recognizing the danger of facile generalizations, it is perhaps useful to summarize certain of this material as follows:

Some women, when they can no longer have children, frequently pour their creative energies into new fields. Margaret Mead, herself an example, characterized this as the female "absolute zest for life."

Religion has been, and to a degree still is, the traditional, accepted direction of such female energy. All churches recognize the tremendous importance and contributions of their female members. These women contribute labor and funds critical to the maintenance and functioning of the churches and their manifold responsibilities.

Traditionally, upper- and middle-class women have also been found in the secular fields — the arts. Museums, concerts, ballet, opera, the theater, and art exhibits have often been supported by local cadres of active, hard-working women of this age group. Such women have also been found as volunteers working for a host of civic organizations, community agencies, and advisory and self-help offices.

Recently, there has been a third trend developing. Some women are now developing their own careers. Postmenopausal women are now returning to school. They want advanced training; they intend to move into the professional, managerial, and business worlds. Their purpose is to be hired, tenured, well-paid staff. Women, in America, are becoming a visible power bloc, not only socially but now also politically and economically.

These generalizations, I believe, are primarily operative for some of our contemporary women. I suggest, however, that this trend will also gradually be reflected among other groups of women making up the heterogeneous American population. Women seem to be on the way to resolving their postmenopausal lives. The female of our species is not only a survivor, she is a developer.

# KAPUTT AT FORTY

THE same cannot necessarily be said for the male of the species. They seem to be the high-risk population. Men after forty seem to become very vulnerable.

Nancy Mayer, in her book on *The Male Mid-Life Crisis* (1978), begins her work by citing the famous *New Yorker* cartoon of the embittered fellow saying: "It's a real American tragedy — *Wunderkind* at twenty, *Übermensch* at thirty, *kaputt* at forty." Contrary to Margaret Mead's description of women at midlife, the male of the species seems to find this a time of crisis.

Joseph Conrad, the Pole who learned English as a foreign language and then went on to write some of the most beautiful and significant English prose of this century, well recognized this problem. In his novel, *Victory,* he wrote, "Forty-five is the age of recklessness for many men, as if in defiance of the decay and death waiting with open arms in the sinister valley at the bottom of the inevitable hill."

Bradford Smith, an insightful Quaker writer, has put it, "No man has reached maturity until he has learned to face the fact of his own death."

For women, the plus-forty characteristic is "the absolute zest for life"; for men the terms are "crisis," "decay," and "death."

Sometimes, this male panic behavior is referred to as the "Gauguin Syndrome." We are all familiar with the Gauguin

Syndrome. It is a form of behavior manifested by a growing number of men during their midlife crisis. Gauguin, a middle-aged stockbroker, left his business, family, and friends and turned to painting in France (he was also part of the Van Gogh crisis). Gauguin later went on to Samoa. Ultimately, his paintings were recognized as those of a world-renowned artist. Unfortunately very few men going through this behavior are as talented as Gauguin.

Others may experience the "Dickens Route." Charles Dickens, during his midlife crisis, left his wife and ten children and went to live with a nineteen-year-old actress.

# THE DANGER ZONE

IT has been advanced that one of the reasons men seem to panic at this age period and women do not, or not as much, is that men are not as prepared for the physical and physiological changes that take place.

Within the normal, expected range of changes that will begin to manifest themselves to all of us are wrinkling and sagging of the skin: under the eyes, at the cheeks, under the jowls, and in the belly. There is a general thickening of the body: flab and fat become more evident. Blood circulation problems seem to be more pronounced and varicose veins and hemorrhoids more troublesome. Hernias start protruding with bumps emerging.

There is an increased sensitivity to heat and cold, particularly cold, at the extremities of the fingers and toes. Skin sores and rashes seem to be more common and to last longer. Stomach disorders such as constipation, diarrhea, and ulcers disturb normal eating habits. Headaches seem to be more frequent. Generalized aches and pains seem to become more common, often along the lower back.

Sleeping habits seem to be changing. It is more difficult to fall asleep. There is more frequent waking up during the night and early wakening in the morning. There seems to develop generalized feeling of being more tired, and feeling weak and weary. There is occasional dizziness.

Night driving seems to be more of a strain and day driving less of a pleasure. Nonspecific feelings of irritability, nervous-

76

ness, loss of self-confidence, doubts, fears, and depression seem to plague the male at odd hours of the day and night. Head hair visibly begins to thin out and disappear. A pronounced receding hairline and baldness start to become reality.

(An ironical development is that as the hair on the head begins to thin out, recede, and disappear, the hair seems to grow more thickly along the sides, at the back, and at the eyebrows, nose and ears. Mother Nature has a delicate sense of humor.)

The bladder is no longer as dependable. There is an increasing need to urinate more frequently, especially in the middle of the night. More frightening, however, is that urinating seems to be more difficult.

Compounding all of the above is the fact that about this same age time, many men seem to undergo dimished sex drive. They no longer seem to have the younger, stronger sex power; impotence becomes less of a joke. "Get it up!" and "Keep it up!" assume far more meaningful significance. Voyeurism, as opposed to active participation, becomes a sexual possibility. The "dirty-old-man" syndrome becomes more understandable. Apparent latent homosexuality may begin to emerge in sexual fantasies.

Liquor addiction may be another concomitant. There develops the need to have a series of strong drinks as soon as possible after the working day. The tendency develops to drink earlier and earlier during the working day. Evenings and weekends may be spent in a state of "alcoholic bliss." Alcohol is needed "to dull my mind and make me forget."

Confronted with all or even some of these changes, many men panic. Contrary to women who have been expecting and experiencing these changes gradually since puberty, men have tended to either deny or ignore them. Suddenly, for men, the midforties changes seem to be a real shock and a precipitous crisis.

All of these and more may be part of the profound physical and physiological changes happening to midlife men.

# THE SHOCK OF RECOGNITION

E RNEST Becker has written that "A full comprehension of the human condition would drive us mad." Perhaps this is applicable to our midlife male.

Very little in a man's life, with its emphasis on physical and sexual prowess, seems to have prepared him for his inevitable decline. The weakening of his physical strength and the diminution of his sexual ability seem to come as an utter shock. It is this shock — this shock of recognition — that seems to make the midlife male so vulnerable.

Women do not seem to go through such a shock. The physical deterioration seems to come as less of a surprise. A few women, it is true, do appear to find this a crisis. They are discernible in their behavior. They stand out; they are uncommon.

Not so for men. This shock of recognition seems to be a far more pronounced male reaction. The behavior, for them, is not uncommon; it can be the norm.

I am, accordingly, targeting in on the plus-forty males. They seem to be the segment of our population most vulnerable. The midlife changes seem to hit them the hardest; they seem to be so utterly unprepared. They tend to react as to a crisis; mental panic and physical illness may result. Even death from a heart attack may be a not uncommon concomitant.

Women survive, even develop. Men crack, even die.

Now these are generalizations. They are not intended to be grim or negative so much as facing potential reality.

The male midlife crisis behavior seems to follow, in my opinion, something of a discernible pattern. All of the details are not yet clear. The variety of crises do not necessarily proceed through all of these stages. I suggest, however, that the pattern which follows is applicable in many instances.

1. The individual begins to experience personal feelings of physical weakening. Disabilities of an acute and chronic nature begin to manifest themselves. Good health can no longer be taken for granted. The body begins to show, sometimes in very dramatic forms, the wear and tear of the years. Normal aging and the excesses of personal abuse (alcohol, tobacco, drugs) begin to reveal themselves.

2. Emotional reactions to these physical problems include anxiety, tension, frustration, and fear. There is a growing awareness of personal impotency to remedy the weakening or to halt the deterioration. There can be a sense of despair as the recognition of the inevitability of it all becomes more and more apparent.

3. There seems to develop a growth of intense personal concern. There is an indifference — almost an antagonism — to the external world. Sometimes the person feels the need for geographic isolation; the person needs to get away from it all. There is an uncommon preoccupation with one's self. There can be an estrangement from usual family and friends. There can be a disinterest in ordinary social relations. Daily personal living seems to narrow down to personal needs, personal problems, and personal goals. There develops an almost exaggerated form of personal tunnel vision.

4. This can lead to aggravated mental states. Personal preoccupation is to be expected, even a certain amount of brooding. Depression is not an uncommon concomitant. There can be more serious manifestations, such as increased heavy drinking, wife/child beatings, and family abandonment. There can be a pronounced intolerance of the behavior of adolescent and young adult offspring. The "last fling," "skirt chasing," and "bald headed row" may be some of the sexual characteristics.

5. This can then proceed in either of two directions. The situation can progressively worsen and the individual can suffer from chronic mental instability or disorderly or unacceptable social behavior.

6. Hopefully, however, the personal crisis can be weathered. The shock taking can end up positively. The midlife person comes to terms with the aging process. The inevitability of the physical and mental aging is accepted.

There is, to some degree, a positive adaptation to the reality.

# AGAIN THE RELIGIOUS FACTOR

INTERESTINGLY, this positive adaptation may be interpreted as a profound religious experience. Some men and women come through such a mid-life crisis and perceive it as having been a religious experience. Some persons may undergo such profound emotions during this period that they can only understand it and express it in religious terms.

God is their salvation. God has spoken to them personally and directly. God has shown them the way. Such persons may undergo what can only be termed a spiritual rebirth. Others may call it a cognitive reorganization. Such persons are God-inspired; they are filled with the Spirit of God.

They have gained new insights; they recognize old wisdom. Sometimes such a person may find a new religion. Another may develop a new variant of an old religion. "Repent!" and "Reform!" and "Judgement!" and "Hell" become essentials of their vocabulary. They have been down the road; they know the dangers. God has saved them. They are now charged to save others.

No longer are they confused and unsure or frightened and insecure. Now they are clear and confident, fired with zeal and determined in righteousness.

Such religious leaders may have been Abraham, Moses, Solomon, Muhammad, Luther, and Buddha. Many of the Old Testament prophets were of this caliber. In certain respects Jesus of Nazareth and Paul of Tarsus would recognize these

81

characteristics. These persons seem to have undergone not dissimilar emotional crises. They were saved by parallel profound religious experiences.

They were tested; they were tempted. They suffered; they endured. Each of them emerged from the fire, as it were, a better person. Each of them had been given a new way to see the world. They were reborn. They had a new explanation for life; they had a new reason for living.

If you know that God has chosen you to be his messenger, his prophet, and his light, then you have been given a new and incredibly important role in life. You have been chosen by God. You will be immortal.

That phrase has relevant implications. Among the many fantasies of a young person, one of the most widespread is that one's career will make one not only important but famous and not only famous but perhaps immortal. The ambitions of Alexander were those of Napoleon and the millions of persons before and since. You will be famous. You will have an outstanding career; your name will live even after you are gone. You will achieve some degree of immortality. You will leave more than your footprint along the stream of time.

One of the factors aggravating the midlife crisis is the realization of the utter fatuousness of such a belief. It is a childish fantasy. It is so naive and so childish as to be embarrassing. You finally begin to realize that your work will not at all be remembered after you are gone. Worse, it will scarcely be recognized while you are still alive. Your career, even a "successful" one, begins to take on an ashes-in-the-mouth aspect. (For example, the philosophers say that any hard worker can achieve a great career, but only the wise person will be satisfied with it.)

During the midlife crisis, the person can undergo a period of seeming career stagnation, even career disequilibrium. The "burnt-out" syndrome is the common description for such a behavior. This need not necessarily be seen as mental instability. More correctly, it may be perceived as career maturation.

The midlife evaluator now places his career in its proper perspective. It is part of his life; it is not his whole life.

Familial relations, particularly the extended family, assume a more meaningful role. They become recognized for what they are: part of one's biological continuity. Your biological family becomes your biological continuity. This is your real immortality. Hitherto the essence of your daily thoughts, concerns, and energies has been your career. Now the central focus of your life becomes your family and its continuity.

During this period men begin to develop affiliative and nurturant roles. Hitherto these have been the domain of the "weaker sex." Men now suddenly recognize them as among the true essentials of life.

Religious behavior may also be modified. As persons mature, ritualistic behavior outside of the home may tend to diminish. Such religious rituals are perceived as no longer necessary; they get in the way of true importance of religion. Religious persons, and even the until-now nonreligious, may begin to manifest an increasing concern with the personal aspects of religion: the relations of person to God, the humanity of person to person, the values of life and the meaning of death. Prayer becomes less ritualistic and far more personal. Persons begin to actually talk to God, directly and quietly. They are no longer content to mutter in unison in response to set chants. Religious practices tend to decline; religious feelings and concerns tend to increase.

There can be, then, a paradoxical situation. We may disengage from one focus of religion, while we reengage with another. The religious experience can be more than a general therapeutic process. The religious experience can be part of the midlife crisis resolution. It can be a positive force waiting to be tapped.

# THE TRIUNE BRAIN

P AUL MacLean coined the term "the triune brain." He postulates that the human
brain in reality constitutes three brains, i. e. three intercon-
nected biological entities.

Each brain, says MacLean, represents a different devel-
opmental stage of human evolution. Each brain has its own
special intelligence; subjectivity; sense of time and space;
memory, motor, and other functions. Not only do the three
brains differ neuroanatomically and functionally, but they
may even contain "strikingly different distributions" of neu-
rochemicals, dopamine, and cholinesterase.

The human brain, explains MacLean, in reality is a three-
layered complex. The first or earliest is the "R-Complex."

The R-Complex constitutes mainly what the neuroan-
atomists call the olfactostriatum, the corpus striatum, and
the globus pallidus. This is the most ancient part of the brain.
It probably evolved several hundred million years ago. We
share this brain in part with the other mammals and reptiles.
For this reason MacLean calls it the reptilian or R-Complex
brain.

Surrounding the R-Complex is the limbic system. It bor-
ders on the underlying brain. We share the limbic system
with the other mammals but, presumably, not in its full development with the reptiles. The limbic system is an advanced evolutionary stage of brain development; it probably
evolved some one hundred fifty million years ago.

The neocortex lies on top of the rest of the brain. The neocortex is clearly the most recent evolutionary development. Similar to other more "advanced" mammals (such as dolphins and whales), we and the other primates have a relatively developed neocortex.

It is these three brains, receiving and reacting, that determine our behavioral perceptions and responses. We humans are subjects to this complex interaction.

Our reptilian level may well be responsible for our most basic rages such as lust, hate, and cruelty. Our kinder and more humane virtures, such as tenderness, kindness, and play may derive from our limbic system, which we share with our primate cousins. Our neocortex, presumably, is responsible for the cultural and intellectual discoveries and inventions unique to our species alone.

The tragedy, of course, is that we are never one brain alone. All three of our brains are alive, alert, active, and ready to rule. Any of the three brains may, at any moment of stimulus, dominate us and determine our behavior. Some of us may even manifest a propensity to be ruled by one or another of the brains. We are all sensitive to this complex reality.

Freud may have initiated this complex trinity when he postulated the human personality to be composed of three interacting forces: the id, ego, and superego. These may correspond, in some degree, to MacLean's own biological distinctions. Transactional analysis may be based upon a similar triage. Called the Child, Parent, and Adult, these three "persons" may interact with each other in a similar relationship.

I suggest that this reasoning has powerful implications for the student of faith healing. It may be postulated, I believe, that the most destructive forces within the human brain, the R-Complex, id, and Child, react negatively under perceived stress and cause harm, illness, and injury to the body. Conversely, the most constructive forces within the human brain, the neocortex, superego, and Adult, can be marshalled to react positively and create health and well-being.

Faith healing, I suggest, is the tapping of this positive force. The deliberate tapping of this positive force is the miracle of faith healing. It is the power of this force that generates and creates the spontaneous remission or the instantaneous healing.

This wonderful force exists as a biological reality within the brain of each and every one of us. It is there waiting to be called upon. It is up to you. You can ignore it; you can utilize it. The utilization of this force is not a mystery — it is a challenge. The challenge is for all of us to use the "human" part of our brain to its fullest capacity.

Faith healing may be merely one example of the incredible powers lying extant within the human brain. This power is lying there, dormant, waiting to be a force for good, waiting to be tapped.

Faith healing — the religious experience as a therapeutic process — is perhaps the most beautiful example of the power for good that can be effected by the union of the biological and mental forces existing within each and every one of us. It is by utilizing our brain to its fullest capacity that we can convert the religious experience into a therapeutic process.

# REFERENCES

Aulen, Gustaf. 1937. *Christus Victor*. (Society for Promoting Christian Knowledge, London.)

Beit-Hallahmi, B. 1977. Curiousity, doubt, and devotion: The belief of psychologists and the psychology of belief, in H. N. Maloney (Editor), *Current Perspectives in the Psychology of Religion*. (Eerdmans, Grand Rapids, Michigan.)

Bonhoeffer, Dietrich. 1959. *The Cost of Discipleship*. Sixth Edition. (SCM Press, London.)

Childs, Brevard. 1979. *Introduction to the Old Testament as Scripture*. (Fortress Press, Philadelphia.)

Huizing, Peter, and William Bassett (Editors). 1974. *Experience of the Spirit*. (Seabury Press, New York.)

Hutch, Richard. 1978. Jonathan Edward's analysis of religious experience. *Journal of Psychology and Theology*. (Vol. 6, No. 2, Spring.)

Schillebeeckx, Edward. 1979. *Jesus: An Experiment in Christology*. Translated by Hubert Hoskins. (Seabury Press, New York.)

Vaux, Peter. 1978. *This Mortal Coil: The Meaning of Health and Disease*. (Harper and Row, New York.)

# AFTERWORD

*Man is the only animal that laughs and weeps, for he is the only animal that is struck with the difference between what things are, and what they ought to be.*

*William Hazlitt (1778-1830)*

I introduced this study of faith healing by recalling the practice of the pre-Columbian mapmakers of Europe — they wrote *Ne Plus Ultra*, "There is no more," after the Straits of Gibraltar.

Subsequent to Columbus and his discoveries of the New World, the mapmakers realized the gravity of their error. They erased the *Ne* and declared *Plus Ultra* — "There is more!"

That is, essentially, the theme of this study of faith healing. I am now at work developing the next stage of these investigations. My new book, tentatively entitled *The Universe of the Mind: Further Explanations into Faith Healing*, will attempt to provide verifiable study and documentation of claimed faith healings. I also hope to develop an improved paradigm to help effect more successful faith-healing circumstances.

The study of faith healing can be the study of a whole new world — demonstrated processes whereby the mind can even more effectively help protect the body, help heal the body. The potential reality and implications of these processes are truly awe-inspiring. We need more scholars, more scientists, more studies, to help us move forward in our explorations.

In this present work, I have attempted to structure and delineate, succinctly, a variety of the manifestations and processes of faith healing reports and practices.

Let us first acknowledge certain givens. It is accepted as a given that a certain number of faith healers may be charlatans, frauds, cheats. It is accepted as a given that a certain percentage of faith-healing claims may be products of wishes, hopes, emotions. It is accepted as a given that a certain degree of claimed successful faith healings may be only temporary or even transitory. Finally, it is accepted as a given that many of our faith healing claims are subjective and anecdotal, rarely documented or verified.

After all of these givens, however, the fact still remains that people across time and space have gone to faith healers and claim to have been healed — and so continue to do and claim, to this day.

The practice is too widespread and too common to be ignored. Faith healing, furthermore, is an essential and important component in one of the most important religions in the entire world — Christianity. Faith healing, accordingly, is an integral part of Western Civilization — critical to the development of medicine as well as religion.

Faith healers claim that they can effect faith healings. Ill persons and their families claim that the faith healings are effective. The sick feel better — pain is made tolerable, diminished, removed. Bodies are restored, cured; life is again made precious.

Based upon my years of fieldwork experience, it is clear to me that faith healing can contain important, critical, and significant elements of reality. Something positive, something therapeutic, some powerful healing force can take place during the religious experience.

This cannot be ignored or denied or derided. The circumstances of faith healing — pronounced mind over body action — warrant and justify large-scale scientific study and research.

With these considerations in mind, let me summarize certain of the reasoning that may help to understand how faith healings can occur. Most healers operate along similar principles. A composite pattern of crisis perception and reaction seems to be a necessary precondition.

As a working generalization: most of us, throughout our lives, are confronted with a variety of perceived stressful situations; most of us cope with most of them, most of the time.

Sometimes we do not.

Life begins to appear to be too hard, too harsh, even cruel. We begin to feel beaten, battered. Repeated blows seem to be pounding us down.

There seems to be no one we can turn to, no one to whom we can tell all of this. No one really cares.

Unable to unload our misery, we become extremely repressed. This worsens the stress, and the two combine to worsen each other. We become depressed, acutely depressed. We feel isolated, alone in a crowded but indifferent world. No one understands; worse, no one cares.

The individual feels caught, trapped — utterly helpless in a sickeningly hopeless situation.

The mind can give up. It is just too much to bear. Mental breakdown can occur. Life can lose its meaning, purpose, value. Suicide can be contemplated; "accidents" can suddenly happen; physical violence, even unto murder, can take place during moments of acute rage.

The body may also respond to this anguish. The body may produce, or allow to be produced, physical illness.

Colds, influenza, pneumonia, and tuberculosis are merely a few of the infectious diseases that have been attributed to stress.

Degenerative diseases may also be engendered. Ulcers, high blood pressure, heart attacks, stroke, even cancer may be physical manifestations of stress-caused mental anguish.

Now, while we do not yet possess a definitely proven cause-and-effect relationship, the broad pattern that I have just sketched seems to be a widely prevalent operational theory.

Let us be very clear that there is no definite proof that every heart attack or cancer case is caused by patient-perceived stress. That indeed could be a cruel charge. It does seem operational, however, that stress may not be an unrelated causal or contributory factor.

Many of our traditionally-trained Western physicians may find the previous material rather unscientific — interesting speculation but quite unproven fact. One can certainly appreciate their position. Trained as they have been with another scientific model — the germ theory — such physicians are often unable to cope with different concepts.

A few physicians, however, are able. Dr. Kenneth Pelletier (1979), in his chapter on "Toward a New Medical Model" (pp. 23-39), joins a small but growing number of physicians who are recognizing that the germ theory, while an excellent foundation upon which to attack infectious diseases, is not sufficient to cope adequately with degenerative diseases such as hypertension or cancer.

The human body, such physicians realize, is not necessarily a machine to be analyzed in terms of its parts — to be diagnosed, dissected, excised, replaced — all while the malfunctioning patient lies there, prone, passive, silent, and grateful.

This mechanistic model is considered to be too limiting, possibly even self-defeating.

Modern medicine, at least the part that Dr. Pelletier calls holistic or humanistic, tries to recognize and deal with the patient as a complex human being, a human being replete with mind as well as body, even spirit and soul.

Many traditional Western physicians might find this to be dangerously unscientific. For perspective, Dr. Pelletier considers how scientific knowledge grows. He cites Thomas Kuhn, who, in his *The Structure of Scientific Revolutions* (1962), noted that every scientific paradigm eventually expands to the limits of its methodology and then ceases to be productive.

At that point there begins to develop an increasing body of information that the paradigm can no longer incorporate or account for. There is the tendency for the traditionalists to deny or ignore the increasing contradictory or unexplained material.

The creative scientists, however, go about trying to construct new paradigms to incorporate or explain these new discoveries, these apparently inexplicable or contradictory materials.

Such creative research generally leaves such scientists open to ridicule and attack. Initially, their theories may be awkward and even inept. This, however, is how science may advance.

Traditionalists would like to imagine that science advances along a smooth upward progression, with each scientist contributing small but essential building blocks. Creative scientists, however, recognize that for science to advance, it is sometimes necessary to posit new directions, new maps. Science, for them, may progress, not necessarily smoothly but rather by a series of quantum leaps, even erratic jumps.

Such creative physicians, for example, attempt to study and explain medically verified cases of spontaneous remission of cancer (Everson and Cole, 1956; Boyd, 1966) by more than attributing the sudden healings to "hormonal influences" or "immune mechanisms."

Such physicians are also aware of the grim humor of their work. During 1975, for example, the people of the United States spent twenty-two billion dollars to purchase alcohol, twelve billion dollars to buy tobacco, and allocated some one-half billion dollars for cancer research. Not surprisingly, in America we have high liquor consumption, tobacco usage, and cancer morbidity and mortality (Goodfield, 1977).

Cancer morbidity and mortality clearly do not occur randomly. There are obviously certain genetic predispositions, environmental conditions, and personal life habits that can help inhibit or aggravate cancer manifestation.

Per present rates, one in four Americans now living, some fifty-six million persons, will have cancer during their lifetime. During the year 1981, almost 420,000 persons in the United States will die of cancer — over one thousand persons a day.

Despite these figures, however, there has been certain progress. One in three persons this year, who learn that they have cancer, will survive five years or more after treatment. When normal life expectancy factors such as dying of heart disease, accidents, and old age diseases are taken into account, 41 percent of cancer patients will survive for five years.

The American Cancer Society, from whom these figures were obtained, emphasizes that many more lives could be saved with early diagnosis and prompt treatment.

Breast cancer continues to be the most frequent type of cancer found in women. In a recent survey conducted by the National Cancer Institute, it was found that "no other medical concern approached the magnitude of response which cancer received."

Of those surveyed, 77 percent of the women listed cancer as the most serious problem facing women today, and one in three women felt that they were very likely, or somewhat likely, to develop the cancer there.

In reality, breast cancer strikes one in eleven women.

When asked for their first impressions about breast cancer, "loss of breast" was mentioned three times more frequently than anything else. This emphasizes, said the report, "the powerful psychological impact of breast cancer" and its association with surgery.

Dr. Vincent T. DeVita, Director of the National Cancer Institute, urged women to take a more active role in regular breast self-examination as an early detection technique.

Early detection is critical. The five-year survival rate after treatment is 85 percent for a localized breast cancer but this drops to 56 percent when the cancer has spread beyond the initial site.

Black and Hispanic women are generally less knowledgeable about breast cancer, self-examination, and treatments than the general population.

Black Americans, in particular, suffer from acute pessimism, myths, and misinformation about cancer. Dr. LaSalle Leffal, Jr., past president of the American Cancer Society, reported that in a survey conducted by their office, black persons think that they are less likely than whites to get cancer; but they are more likely to think that if they do get cancer it will be fatal.

"Blacks are not familiar with the early signs of cancer and since they are not," said Dr. Leffal, "they tend not to seek medical care." Delayed detection leads to delayed diagnosis and this, in turn, leads to increased mortality.

The overall cancer incidence rate for whites has dropped 3 percent over the past quarter century; the overall cancer incidence rate for blacks over the same period has increased 8 percent.

Cancer mortality rates are also accordingly higher for blacks than whites. According to Dr. Leffal, the number of cancer deaths in blacks is up 26 percent over the last two decades. This is about five times the increase over the same period for whites.

Clearly, normal accepted cancer awareness and self-examination could help in early cancer detection, diagnosis, and treatment among blacks as it has among whites.

Lack of knowledge, stereotyping, fear, and fatalism may all play critical roles in helping to make cancer such a serious problem among American blacks.

Stress may well be a crucial negative force. According to Dr. David Sobell, Chief of Preventive Medicine at San Francisco's Kaiser-Permanent Medical Center, stressors can cause changes in the hypothalamus — a tiny region of the brain that stimulates hormone secretion from the pituitary and other glands. The hypothalamus is linked to the immune system in ways still not fully understood.

Under stress, humans, as other animals, secrete hormones that put the body on the alert, increasing heart rate, blood pressure, and respiration. A prolonged hormonal tide, however, could work adversely, reducing or weakening the body's natural immunity mechanisms, opening the body to infectious as well as degenerative diseases (Ingber, 1981).

Faith healing may well be a deliberate reversal of this negative trend; a deliberate stimulating of positive, therapeutic forces. It is perhaps unfortunate that the American medical profession does not allow for more therapeutic latitude.

According to Robert Eagle (1980), England is unusually tolerant of unorthodox medicine. Unlike France and the United States where persons who practice medicine without a state recognized qualification can be prosecuted as quacks, English Common Law allows anyone to set up in medical business.

What is important to note, states Mr. Eagle, is that England is a country where medical treatment is free, yet hundreds of thousands of patients prefer to pay for the additional services of non-Western trained healers and therapists. Advancing medical science, says the author, should have made these practitioners redundant, "but they flourish and grow."

England, again, may well be in the forefront of medical and scientific progress.

In this book after citing a number of case studies illustrating the realities of faith healing, demonstrations of the power of the mind over the body, and the nature of much of our present day degenerative disorders, I then went on to delineate field reports of personal faith healing services.

Faith healing, I emphasized, is a cross-cultural phenomenon found, to some degree, in every society of the world since the appearance of our species. Contrary to popular opinion, the oldest profession in the world is probably that of the faith healer. The eminent physician Sir William Osler noted that as late as this century faith played an essential role in the healing process, even in England and America.

Traditionally, faith healing has been delineated as the acceptance and utilization of supernatural powers to help establish and ensure the healing process. Faith healing, in addition to its dependence on the supernatural, has also included some degree of knowledge and utilization of medical expertise, including the use of local plant and animal potions, purges and emetics, sweating, bleeding, massaging, even elementary obstetrics and surgery. The local faith healer, referred to in Western terms as the *medicine man, shaman,* or *witch doctor,* is in reality the medium to help induce the supernatural powers to provide their services and to help them exorcise the evil spirit, power, or mass temporarily invading the victim's body.

The early civilizations of Sumeria, Egypt, India, and China, as well as the later Aztec, Maya, and Inca Civilizations, all demonstrated technical and philosophical variations of this basic theme. The Old Testament records traditional Semitic concepts and practices of faith healing even as the Jews were developing their strict monotheistic belief. Greco-Roman medicine manifested a mixture of traditional Semitic and Indo-European faith healing practices, e.g. the temples to Aesclepius, the god of Healing, and slowly emerging biophysiological techniques for diagnosis and treatment, e.g. the school of Hippocrates.

The New Testament describes the numerous and dramatic healings performed by Jesus. Tillich argues that the ideal *soter* (savior) of that period in Judaism was the healer, "who makes healthy and whole." According to Tillich, the New Testament reports of healing should not be taken as mere miracles but rather as proof demonstrating Jesus as the True Savior, the Universal Healer. Jesus was the Christ by virtue of his healings.

Christianity, says Tillich, is unique among the world religions in that it places the healing powers of its founder as part of the demonstrated proof of his legitimacy. Christianity makes faith healing a central theme within the religion, an integral part of its theology, an essential component of its practice.

The history of Christianity has been, and still is, the unique record of sanctioned and sanctified faith healing.

Contemporary Christianity continues to manifest this emphasis, and radio and television have helped to enhance and dramatize this practice even more popularly, even amidst modern medicine.

Derived from my research and field studies, I went on to try and abstract from this mass of material a proposed paradigm.

Essentials of a faith-healing service usually include (1) the appropriate religious/therapeutic setting, (2) a "cloud of witnesses" to support and encourage the therapeutic activity, (3) a healer — usually an inspiring Father or Mother figure, (4) a healee — who must truly desire to be healed (never a given). The healee must be willing to (5) publicly confess sins and errors in order that the healer can initiate a healing comprising (6) the pronouncement of a positive prognosis, (7) the healer touches, holds, strokes the patient, often with holy water or oil, and then the healer (8) shouts the positive commandment that the healing has been effected.

In a surprising number of cases, that is precisely what is claimed to have taken place — a successful faith healing.

I have suggested that the faith healing that may take place is really a manifestation of what I refer to as telescoped time therapy — an incredibly powerful life force potential concerning which we know virtually nothing.

Finally, I suggest that the ethical contract may be the rationale that enables the positive interaction of religion and medicine. The ethical contract reasoning may well operate as a predictive factor in enabling us to understand which type of persons are most likely to be healed.

I have tried to delineate all of this in as clear and succinct a manner as possible, yet I am aware of how much more there is to understand. I am painfully aware of how much more there is yet to explore.

That, however, is the great challenge. The purpose of exploration, wrote T. S. Eliot, is really to allow us to understand the beginning "and know the place for the first time" (from "Little Gidding" in *Four Quartets*). The full exploration of faith healing, I suggest, may help us better comprehend ourselves and thus live fuller and healthier lives.

This book can help provide you with understandings and processes as to how you can make faith healing work for you.

## REFERENCES

Boyd, William. 1966. *The Spontaneous Remission of Cancer.* (Thomas, Springfield.)

Eagle, Robert. 1980. Alternative medicine. *The Listener, 2680:* 394-95.

Everson, Tilden C. and Warren H. Cole. 1956. *Spontaneous Remission of Cancer.* (W.B. Saunders, Philadelphia.)

Goodfield, June. 1977. Humanity in science: a perspective and a plea. *Science, 198:* 580-85.

Ingber, Dina. 1981. Ravages of stress. *Science Digest, 10:* 61.

Kuhn, Thomas. 1962. *The Structure of Scientific Revolutions.* (University of Chicago Press, Chicago.)

Pelletier, Kenneth. 1979. *Holistic Medicine.* (Delacorte Press, New York.)

# ANNOTATED BIBLIOGRAPHY

Antonovsky, Aaron. 1979. *Health, Stress, and Coping: New Perspectives on Mental and Physical Well-Being.* (Jossey-Bass, Inc., San Francisco.)

Antonovsky has written a detailed sociocultural investigation of the circumstances of health. After summarizing a U. S. National Health Survey revealing that at least one-third of Americans suffer from some morbid pathological condition at any given time, Antonovsky asks, "So who stays healthy?" His general theory of health and analysis of major concepts of health and ill-health is written in the traditional sociological manner but contains excellent material and merits serious study.

Brod, Max. 1960. *Franz Kafka: A Biography.* Second Enlarged Edition. (Schocken Books, New York.)

This can serve as a dramatic accounting of how a literary genius seemed to turn his mind to resolve perceived social problems through physical illness and ultimate death. An interesting personal recording, this can be a reference to help understand other artistic "tragedies."

Cannon, W. B. 1939. *The Wisdom of the Body.* (W. W. Norton and Company, New York.)

An outstanding classic that initiated much of contemporary thinking about human physiology and stress and the need to establish and maintain proper functioning — what Cannon called "homeostasis" — this is still a work well worth studying.

Carrel, Alexis. 1950. *Journey to Lourdes.* (Harper and Sons, New York.)

This is a recent edition of the experiences that Dr. Carrel underwent as he accompanied Marie Bailly on her supposed last rites to Lourdes.

Carrington, Hereward. 1935. *Loaves and Fishes.* (Charles Scribner's Sons, New York.)

This work is in the tradition of Christian portrayal and acceptance of the healing ministry of Jesus Christ. It is important to read such work in order to understand Christian faith healing services.

Cousins, Norman. 1979. *Anatomy of an Illness as Perceived by the Patient: Reflections on Healing and Regeneration.* (W. W. Norton and Co., New York.)

The author, former editor of the *Saturday Review*, has written an interesting personal account of his recovery from a crippling and supposedly irreversible disease. The life-force may be the most underrecognized energy on earth, and Cousins has provided anecdotal material to stimulate thought and hope. Rene Dubos has written an extremely helpful Introduction to accompany Cousins. This is certainly recommended reading as an introduction to the field.

Dittes, James E. 1973. *Bias and the Pious.* (Augsberg Publishing House, Minneapolis.)

This is a beautifully written, clearly presented analysis of the problems associated with varieties of prejudice among the religious orthodox. It has strong implications for the study of religion and healing.

Flammonde, Paris. 1974. *The Mystic Healers.* (Stein and Day, New York.)

This work, along with the studies of Harrell and Meek, provide a very useful introduction to the important study of religion and healing.

Frankl, Viktor E. 1975. *The Unconscious God: Psychotherapy and Theology.* Simon and Schuster, New York.)

Viktor Frankl here considerably updates and expands his 1963 book *From Death Camp to Existentialism.* Frankl draws on his personal experiences of surviving the Holocaust and his development as a psychiatrist. In conceiving the practice of logotherapy, Frankl attempts to unite these two phenomena toward a meaningful therapy.

Galton, Lawrence. 1979. *You May Not Need a Psychiatrist: How Your Body May Control Your Mind.* (Simon and Schuster, New York.)

Galton is the author of over a dozen popularly written books of a medical nature. He writes clearly and presents his material in an easy-to-read, anecdotal manner. This book argues that perhaps quite a bit of "mental illness" may be just bad diagnosis; the problem may really be undetected physical disorders that are affecting the behavior.

Group for the Advancement of Psychiatry. 1960. *Psychiatry and Religion: Some Steps Toward Mutual Understanding and Usefulness.* (Report No. 48, New York.)

The critical study of the factors of psychiatry and religion, and their interaction, merits objective and unprejudiced research. It is unfortunate that too much of the material presently available is still too biased to be utilized.

The 1960 GAP recommendations are still appropriate. An update on the problem is the Fall, 1978 issue of *The Journal of Psychology and Judaism* (Vol. III, No. 1), which devotes its entire issue to "Mystics and Medics: A Comparison of Mystical and Psychotherapeutic Encounters."

Harrell, David Edwin, Jr. 1975. *Things are Possible: The Healing and Charismatic Revivals in Modern America.* (Indiana University Press, Bloomington.)

Harrell has written a scholarly survey of previous and contemporary faith healing religious movements. This is a very useful presentation.

Kelsey, Morton T. 1973. *Healing and Christianity in Ancient Thought and Modern Times.* (Harper and Row, New York.)

Among the many books on this subject Kelsey, from the University of Notre Dame, has written one of the more analytical studies of the long interaction between Christianity and healing. It is also something of a personal testament. As Kelsey states, "I have seen the things of which I write."

LaBarre, Weston. 1978. *The Ghost Dance: Origins of Religion.* Third Printing. (Dell Publishing Company, New York.)

LaBarre has written a fascinating tour de force delineating psychological, historical, and anthropological manifestations of religion. LaBarre provides a broad time and space description and analysis of critical world religions and their interaction. The variety of religious leaders and their practices are a central theme of the work.

Lasko, Keith Alan. 1980. *The Great Billion Dollar Medical Swindle.* (Bobbs-Merrill, New York.)

Lasko, a physician in private practice in California, writes a blasting indictment of his own profession. He states that his is a "true expose of the whole rotten medical profession" (p. xv) because "never before in history has the medical profession been so corrupt." (p. xvi). *Inter alia* he calls the psychiatrist "the absurd healer," and he claims that physicians have turned cancer into a lucrative industry. Obviously a challenging and provocative writer, Lasko provides an interesting perspective on the profession of healers.

LeShan, Lawrence. 1977. *You Can Fight for Your Life: Emotional Factors in the Causation of Disease.* (M. Evans & Company, New York.)

LeShan has worked long and hard in studying the causal factors between emotions and disease. This is a positive, up-beat book that provides an optimistic challenge to the reader.

Lygre, David G. 1979. *Life Manipulation from Test-Tube Babies to Aging.* (Walker and Company, New York.)

Lygre has collected an interesting and useful series of case studies demonstrating recent medical techniques for modifying and prolonging life. He provides a good background for helping to understand modern medical "breakthroughs."

Lynch, James T. 1977. *The Broken Heart: The Medical Consequences of Loneliness.* (Basic Books, New York.)

While much of this may already be known, or assumed, Lynch brings it all together and provides useful documented, contemporary, material.

MacLean, Paul D. 1973. *Triune Concepts of the Brain and Behavior.* (University of Toronto Press, Toronto.)

Dr. MacLean has developed a brilliant exposition of brain evolution and human behavior. This may well be a landmark publication.

Mayer, Nancy. 1978. *The Male Mid-Life Crisis: Fresh Starts After Forty.* (Doubleday & Company, New York.)

She begins with the famous *New Yorker* cartoon of the embittered fellow saying, "It's a real American tragedy — *Wunderkind* at twenty, *Übermensch* at thirty, *kaputt* at forty," and goes on in a lively and anecdotal manner to consider the postforty male. If the reader has not done much previous reading about the subject, this can be a very useful introduction.

Meek, George W. (Editor). 1977. *Healers and the Healing Process.* (Theosophical Publishing House, Wheaton, Illinois.)

Meek has written and incorporated material concerning a variety of contemporary faith healers. He has a very personal approach to the subject but tries to be a careful and honest reporter.

Myer, Donald. 1965. *The Positive Thinkers.* (Doubleday & Company, New York.)

This is a well-written summary concerning a variety of popular "positive thinkers" and their theories, arguments, techniques, and practices. It is an interesting collection and provides a useful historical perspective.

Pelletier, Kenneth R. 1977. *Mind as Healer, Mind as Slayer.* (Delta Books, New York.)

Pelletier has assembled a good amount of data demonstrating the constructive and destructive processes of the human mind. His work is challenging and provides excellent material for study.

Regush, Nicholas M. 1977. *Frontiers of Healing: New Dimensions in Parapsychology.* (Avon Books, New York.)

In addition to a Foreword containing a historical summary and philosophical statement by the Academy of Parapsychology and Medicine, the book contains nineteen papers on processes of healing through psychic powers. As such, it presents a panorama of speculations and speculators. This is a useful, recent publication representing this healing orientation.

Restak, Richard M. 1979. *The Brain: The Last Frontier.* (Doubleday & Company, Inc., New York.)

This is a well-written and clearly reasoned presentation that can be utilized along with other references cited in this annotated bibliography. Careful students will be interested in comparing the different emphases on techniques and processes for future research.

Sagon, Carl. 1977. *The Dragons of Eden.* (Ballantine Books, New York.)

Professor Sagan has written a popular but soundly documented accounting and updating of the developing science of our species. This can provide an excellent introduction to the systematic study of the subject.

Sandner, Donald. 1979. *Navajo Symbols of Healing.* (Harcourt Brace Jovanovich, New York.)

Among the many studies of specific cultures and their processes of healing, this is a good study of a local American Indian tribe, the Navajo, which still utilizes certain of the traditional medicines and practices.

Scarf, Maggie. 1980. Images that heal: a doubtful idea whose time has come. *Psychology Today.* (Vol. 14, No. 4, September, 1980, p. 32-46.)

Scarf has written a most-recent evaluation of the clinic and practice of Simonton and his colleagues. This should be read in conjunction with their book.

Selye, Hans. 1956. *The Stress of Life.* (McGraw-Hill, New York.)

Along with Cannon's *The Wisdom of the Body,* this is another of those modern classics often referred to but seldom read. Selye, writing clearly and carefully, demonstrates how emotions such as frustration or suppressed rage can lead to adrenal exhaustion, which can result in bodily ailments. Selye details certain of the ill-effects of negative emotions on body chemistry. He has popularized the recognition of the importance of stress as a significant factor in causing illness and inhibiting therapeutic recovery.

Simonton, O. Carl, Stephanie Matthews-Simonton, and James Creighton. 1978. *Getting Well Again: A Step-by-Step Self-Help Guide to Overcoming Cancer for Patients and their Families.* (J. P. Tarcher, Los Angeles.)

This is a curiously disappointing book by one of the contemporary leaders of the self-imaging cancer therapy process. The book is certainly worth reading, but Simonton has still to write the book delineating his medical regimen.

Sobel, David S. (Editor). 1979. *Ways of Health: Holistic Approaches to Ancient and Contemporary Medicine.* (Harcourt Brace Jovanovich, New York.)

Sobel has prepared a very readable collection of twenty essays by a variety of scholars and scientists. Rene Dubos writes in the Preface that "scientific medicine" is not yet sufficiently "scientific," and he argues for a more open approach to traditional medical practices.

Stone, George C., Frances Cohen, Nancy E. Adler, and Associates. 1979. *Health Psychology: A Handbook: Theories, Applications, and Challenges of a Psychological Approach to the Health Care System.* (Jossey-Bass, Inc., San Francisco.)

In this thick compendium is assembled much of current thinking concerning the applications of psychology to help improve understanding of health and illness. Analysis is also provided to help improve our cumbersome and expensive health care system. This can be a useful reference text.

Thomas, Lewis. 1978. *The Medusa and the Snail: More Notes of a Biology Watcher.* (Viking, New York.)

Lewis Thomas, President of the Memorial Sloan-Kettering Cancer Center in New York, writes gracefully and thoughtfully on a variety of relevant health issues. Warts, he notes, are "one of the great mystifications of science." With the correct thoughts, or suggestion, warts can be ordered off the skin, made to go away. "This," declares Thomas, "is absolutely astonishing." Faith healing, implies Thomas, should receive as much serious medical attention as cloning or recombinant DNA or endorphin or acupuncture.

Tillich, Paul. 1967. The meaning of health. Pp. 3-12 in David Belgum, Editor. *Religion and Medicine.* (Iowa State Press. Ames.)

Tillich, as an outstanding theologian, here applies his religious thinking to the deeper meanings of health. This is a fruitful reasoning of these interactions between the two critical realities.

Torrey, E. Fuller. 1972. *The Mind Game: Witch Doctors and Psychiatrists.* (Emerson Hall, New York.)

Torrey's thesis is that "witch doctors and psychiatrists are really the same behind their exterior mask or pipe." Torrey is challenging, provocative, and makes a good argument.

Weatherhead, Leslie D. 1951. *Psychology, Religion, and Healing.* (Abingdon-Cokesbury, New York.)

Along with the later work of Kelsey (1973), Weatherhead has written a detailed and documented history of the long interaction of these three phenomena. The two works should be read together for comparative and integrative learning.

White, John. 1977. *Daring to Draw Near: People in Prayer.* (Intervarsity Press, Downers Grove, Illinois.)

White, Professor of Psychiatry at the University of Manitoba, is one of the few of his profession who publicly advocates the use of prayer as a positive force for therapy. His stand on religion is uncommon among the practitioners of psychiatry.

# INDEX